FAM.

Kathy Murphy

Manchester into
and beyond
World War II

Kathy's true life experiences into and through her teenage years

First Edition: Family Ties
First published in Great Britain in 2010 by:
Indigo Dreams Publishing
132 Hinckley Road
Stoney Stanton
Leics
LE9 4LN

www.indigodreams.co.uk

Kathy Murphy has asserted her right under the Copyright, Designs and Patents Act 1988 to be identified as the author of this work.
©2010 Kathy Murphy

ISBN 978-1-907401-30-5

British Library Cataloguing in Publication Data. A CIP record for this book can be obtained from the British Library.

This book is sold subject to the condition that it shall not, by way of trade or otherwise, be lent, re-sold, hired out, or otherwise circulated without the author's and publisher's prior consent in any form of binding or cover other than that in which it is published and without a similar condition including this condition being imposed on the subsequent purchaser.

Designed and typeset in Goudy Old Style by Indigo Dreams.
Cover design by Ronnie Goodyer at Indigo Dreams.

Printed and bound in Great Britain by Imprint Academic, Exeter

Kathy Murphy (nee Boulger) was born in Manchester, where (apart from a brief period of evacuation) she lived with her parents and elder brother. She was a teenager during the Second World War and became a secretary in a leading Manchester City firm of solicitors. Having retired to France with her husband several years' ago, she is now into a new career as a writer. Only after she'd recorded her recollections spanning the period from pre-war days up to newly married life, did she realise how close knit families were then when compared with modern U.K. lifestyles. Hence the title - 'Family Ties'.

DEDICATION

To Roy for his stubbornness, pig-headedness and support which helped make this possible

CONTENTS

Introduction		8
Chapter 1	Poverty – then and now	10
Chapter 2	Milking Life – the community pinta	21
Chapter 3	Abandoned – evacuation to the Isle of Man	27
Chapter 4	The Blitz – outliving the bombs	33
Chapter 5	Wartime Living – for a teenager	43
Chapter 6	Employment – an early start	50
Chapter 7	Entertaining – war time recreation	60
Chapter 8	Fashion – of the times	72
Chapter 9	Appearance – visual aids and products	90
Chapter 10	Music – favourites of the time	99

FAMILY TIES

Kathy Murphy

INTRODUCTION

Although born in Manchester in July 1927, it has taken me this long to realise that my experiences were the experiences of many in England and elsewhere, who grew up during the Second World War. It is still difficult to fully understand what 'World War' - the world war that involved me - meant, and might mean today.

In the nineteen thirties, class divisions existed that would make a mockery of the attempts at contrasting rich and poor in what is now twenty first century 'United Kingdom'. My family were middle class, although our status would define us as poor today. I have tried in the first Chapters to set the scene as it existed during my infancy. Then I go on to record one of the most traumatic experiences of my early years - evacuation. I was lucky. Many of my age weren't and they all have stories to tell.

Until the start of 'the War', my childhood was a happy one with lots of aunts, uncles and cousins to visit. My mother had five brothers and five sisters, all but two married with families. We were close, most weekends being spent either visiting or receiving one or other of them. Once or twice a fortnight I went with Mum to see her Father. His wife, my Grandmother had died when I was two. He had a waxed moustache (popular at the time) and I was always required to give him a kiss. Only later, after his death, did I discover he was Austrian and my Grandmother German.

Rescued by my parents from evacuation after only a short period, I returned to a strange, uncertain world. History will record the War as being from 1939 to 1945, and people were dying during the whole of that time. Yet in Manchester, indeed throughout England, there was nothing but expectation during the first year or so. Yes we were warned, and our Government took steps, including evacuation, but the conflict was remote, like, for example, the war in Afghanistan. Our soldiers were dying, but we weren't.

Then came the killing. London, Liverpool, Coventry, Birmingham, Bristol and elsewhere, saw houses, offices, factories, roads, railways wiped out. Thousands of people, just like my parents, or children like me, were killed. It was a lottery whether we lived or died. Sometimes we would hear the bombs coming, almost always the approach of the aircraft and the firing of our guns, embedded in concrete around our most vulnerable areas, trying to destroy the enemy. There was a battery of ack-ack guns based alongside a railway line close to us.

From the dreaded warning of the air raid siren, which bade us take cover, to the different note which told us the raid was over, there was noise. Each time it happened – sometimes more than once a night, or in daytime, there was that noise – the guns of our men, firing at hidden targets, the never to be forgotten drone of the bombers, the whistles as the bombs descended, the thud as they hit, the explosions and the fires.

We were lucky in our area, our house, our street (we called it an Avenue because the houses were semi-detached, unlike 'streets' nearer the centre, where they were terraced – class distinction again). We survived without a hit.

And that was a World War. It involved Europe, then Japan and America with other countries joining in to help. It was probably the last time rules of combat, developed over centuries, held firm. Even then the concept of men confronting men began to crumble, with command of the air promising destruction far beyond the battlefield.

That was the background against which I grew up to mature into a working girl and eventually a mother.

K.M. 2010

CHAPTER 1

POVERTY

The poor then

My experience through life has taught me that poverty is relative. In my early childhood, before the War, I never even thought about it, although I did notice a difference when I went to my Grandfather's house in the Manchester district called Moston or when we called on three or four of my other relations. I had to go out into their back yards to use the toilet. Like most in the street, the little brick built cubicles were next to their coal sheds, with whitewashed insides. I now know that in some streets there was only double seated accommodation, sometimes shared by more than one household. Fortunately, as I say, my relatives had their own exclusive 'one at a time' facility which could actually be flushed into a sewer.

I can still picture the wooden holder mounted on the wall, offering a white, shiny, hard roll of toilet paper. During the War that was a luxury, often difficult to get. The alternative was newspaper. In the more considerate households this was cut into squares with a piece of string threaded through a hole in one corner to produce several sheets. These were hung from a nail on the wall. I'm pleased to say print in those days was far less smudgy and never left blackened hands or other parts of the anatomy. Just as well as there were no immediately available hand-washing facilities. Indeed the houses themselves didn't have running hot water and depended on gas for lighting. Electricity had yet to reach them

In our home, we never felt we were rich. In fact we weren't and survival was often a struggle, but we always had an inside toilet, hot and cold water as did most of my Mother's friends in Burnage and Levenshulme. The class system certainly existed and areas such as Chorlton-on-Medlock, Ardwick, Ancoats and Collyhurst were referred to as districts for the poor, remote from our way of life. Occupying rows of terraced houses, crammed together by Landlords providing only the basic facilities, workers were forced to clatter along cobbled streets in their clogs or heavy boots to survive sometimes horrific employment conditions in the adjacent mills. Even so, the majority of housewives, indeed the great majority, took pride in their homes. Most had pristine net curtains with winter and summer drapes. The doorsteps and window sills were constantly rubbed with a cream or white stone which the rag and bone man would give in exchange for some old clothing. The resulting spotless surfaces stood out in stark contrast to the coatings of soot from the mill chimneys that blackened the brickwork.

When I was young there were no contraception pills and families were much larger. Many men could not do skilled jobs. Having left school at the age of fourteen few had the ability to seek further education to improve their prospects, not that funds were readily available if they could have done. As soon as the children started employment, throughout their teens and beyond, they had to contribute to the family income with work often so exhausting and hours so long, evening classes were impossible. The unemployed received a few shillings a week dole money whilst they tried to find labouring jobs, but modern day family allowances and other benefits didn't exist.

The breadwinner of a poor family had to provide money for the rent and with what was left buy the most basic food items to feed often up to 10 children sleeping four or more to a bed. Mothers would go out cleaning or take in washing to make a few extra shillings (the weekly total rarely reached anything like ten shillings (50p). Young members of the family would collect empty bottles and take them back to the grocers to get one or two old pennies. They would collect firewood off tips and the older ones would go to the entrance of the colliery to grab any pieces of coal which dropped off the lorries. They would seek out and shovel up some of the dust, or 'slack' as we called it.

Little carts made out of orange boxes often fitted with old pram wheels found on the dump would be used to transport home the coal or firewood - the only method of heating in their often very damp houses. In contrast my Dad was able to afford two bags of fuel each week so I never had to suffer living totally without warmth from a coal fire. The poorer children would seek jobs to do for the better off, sometimes earning six pence (2.5 pence) which would immediately be handed to their mother. As a reward she would try to produce a special, nourishing meal for the whole family. To them it was the equivalent of a slap-up feed in a posh restaurant, or perhaps more likely, a twenty first century trip to a McDonalds or to other fast food, perhaps less healthy alternatives.

Thinking back my Dad must have started off closer than we ever were to the poorest in Manchester. To some extent he was an example of the rewards determination to win a better life can achieve. He did go to evening classes. He avoided a lifetime of virtual slavery in the mills and by the time the Second World War was over had achieved a lifestyle far beyond the dreams of many at that time.

With their homes being built close to the factories in which the poorer families were destined to work, they were even more vulnerable during times of conflict. These factories (they were always called 'mills') were often requisitioned by the Government to manufacture armaments necessary for the war effort, so were targets for enemy bombers. Precision bombing didn't exist, and whole rows of houses suffered. Like the peoples of Afghanistan and Iraq of more recent times, thousands of British citizens were wiped out by the Second World War.

The poor now

I often think the ease with which we accept our freedom and opportunities to enjoy ready meals, take-away and restaurant fare has destroyed the pleasure those children experienced as a result of their labours. I say again, poverty is relative. To-day in the U.K. it is painted as the difficulty in surviving on the Family Allowance, or State Pension plus the many hand-outs available to assist those who struggle to live in accommodation that would have placed them high above the nineteen thirties and forties poor of Manchester. The workers of that era would have survived on the food scraps dumped by their counterparts in many a modern refuse bin.

I suppose Mother, Father, my Brother and I - our family during the war years - would be classified poor by modern standards. We didn't have a larder, and fridges were a luxury beyond normal households. The only cool place was under the stairs where the milk, butter and other produce were kept. Indeed we would probably have been classified extremely poor in comparison to those interviewed by current day correspondents. They can be seen in well furnished, comfortable living rooms, suffering under the burden of credit card debts which threaten repossession of the large television in the corner and a mobile phone on the shelf above the central heating radiator. The kitchen will have an electric or gas cooker possibly with timer and fan oven. There's likely to be a fridge, a washing machine, maybe a micro wave, a toaster, electric kettle, and perhaps even a dishwasher. Running hot water might come from a boiler in a cupboard used to air clothes. There would be toilet paper in the toilet, probably soft tissue, perhaps a low level flush and a shower. Coal fires and dirty chimneys, unheated rooms are replaced by automatic, insulated warmth requiring no more effort than a coin in the meter, often not even that.

Apart from the cooker, we had none of these facilities, but we weren't poor. And we were happy. We also had greater respect for what we had, including food. Meal times were an event to be shared round a table. Economics called for the making of tasty meals at home from simple, in season produce. We knew what ingredients were in them. I don't advocate that we should return to the deprivations of those days. Neither do I criticise the help available to the poor of the twenty first century, or the reasonable use of State funds, but, to me, it is unfortunate that, as a result, community spirit appears to have suffered; attitudes to have deteriorated. Few seem now to have the guidance my granddaughter received from her Mother, ensuring she can and does produce an appetising balanced meal for the family. From the end of the twentieth century onwards many young people have been deprived of family based education in the elements of life, having to rely on school tuition, with cooking often no more than an option subject, if indeed it exists at all.

1950s marriage

I keep going on about poverty being relative. This is not just a contrast between now and the nineteen forties' years of war. Even the last of rationing was over when I got married in 1955. That was perhaps the time of my biggest reality check, starting just a few months before the ceremony. My future husband and I had put down a five per cent deposit on a new house which was being built at Hazel Grove, Stockport. It was to be a three bedroom semi with two reception rooms, kitchen, bathroom and a nice size garden backing onto the playing fields of a grammar school. The price was £1,800 and we had an offer of a ninety five per cent Mortgage from Manchester Corporation at 5½% interest (100% mortgages were virtually non-existent then).

About a couple of months before the Wedding we received a letter saying that due to increases an extra £20 would be added to the purchase price. Three weeks later we were told that another £23 would be added. The house was only at ground floor level and my Father warned that the price was likely to go up further before completion. In today's property market these figures must seem very low until you consider we were only earning £10 a week between us. We decided it would be sensible to withdraw from the purchase and recover our deposit.

That left us getting married with nowhere to live. My boss at the time, Mr. Moon, sensing there was something wrong, talked to my Father who worked in the same solicitor's office as Managing Clerk. Mr. Moon was a director in three private companies which between them owned several hundred terraced houses. It was a time when private landlords did most of the letting, with council houses still to really make their mark. The

Company Secretary reported that a mill worker's dwelling had just become empty and he offered it to us.

Warned that it would need decorating, that night my Father took us to see it. One of a terrace in Middleton Junction, it had the Co-operative Wholesale Jam Factory opposite. The entrance led to a small passage with a door to the right into the front room, a reasonably sized lounge with a sash window. Next came the stairs and then another doorway into a second large sized room. This had a recess in the corner near the window, accommodating an old gas stove and a moulded concrete slab of a sink. We went upstairs to discover one room with two windows facing the front and another which had a bath but no hot water or toilet. My Dad explained that was in the back yard. What he didn't warn us was what kind of toilet it was.

True to custom, there it was, next to the coal shed. I was told it was a 'tippler'. At the end of a big drop was a flat metal plate. There was no flush or running water and when the contents of the pan got to a certain weight the plate, which was on a pivot, 'tippled', depositing the effluent into the sewer. I'd got to twenty seven years of age, cocooned in a lower middle class household never having had to contend with such a disgusting piece of equipment. We only had in the bank £127, but like many other couples at the time, we were desperate for somewhere to live. So I gratefully thanked my boss for the offer but did wonder if he had ever used a 'tippler'.

Needless to say, I poured many bottles of the strongest disinfectant I could buy down that toilet. Every night for the next few weeks before the wedding, we went up to number 64 Mills Hill Road straight from work. When we'd finished painting and decorating we felt proud of our first home. With some of the money left from the deposit for the new house and my Father's help, we replaced the old sink in the kitchen with one of the new types and our greatest asset was a gas geezer fitted above it. Most of the time, this gave us running hot water through a short, narrow curved pipe hovering over it.

Our first move

We lived at Number 64 for nine months before my Father told me that Number 10 further up the road had become vacant. It had three bedrooms and we think might have originally housed one of the managers or factory foremen. It was certainly up-market from Number 64 and as I had just discovered I was pregnant, it seemed a good move. Nevertheless, a lady had lived in it for some 50 years, and as can be expected it was not in a good state.

Like many of these bay windowed type houses it looked very nice from the outside. There was a hall with a door leading into a good sized lounge. It had two alcoves on either side of the fireplace. At the end of the hall there was another good sized room used as the dining room and opposite another door. This led into a pantry under the stairs and a final door from the hall opened into the kitchen. It had a sink, and to our excitement, hot water supplied from an immersion heater in a tank. The only other item was a small freestanding cupboard. We added another, giving a generous amount of storage space topped by two drawers and a formica work surface. Later we acquired a kitchen cabinet, this still being very popular at the time.

The yard at the back was reasonable in size with a two foot high raised flower bed. We looked at the loo, next to the coal shed as usual, expecting the worst, but found a flush toilet.

Outside the back gate was a wide entry and many occupants had built sheds, some the size of garages. They stood on a level strip of land opposite, before it sloped down to the Canal. After a year or two, my husband was supplied with a car for his work, and we parked it on a concrete standing in this area.

Upstairs were two good sized rooms with a third containing a bath and hand basin again with hot and cold water, but, of course, no toilet. The accommodation was indeed luxurious compared to No. 64, in spite of the fact that everywhere needed decorating.

We'd been engaged for two and a half years before our marriage, and during our engagement we saw a dining room suite we liked in a local large furniture store called Wade & Co. We were admiring this, imagining it as part of our future, but when approached by the salesman, had to admit we didn't plan to marry for another eighteen months. After a lengthy discussion the store agreed to hold it in their warehouse as long as I went in every week to pay something off the price. I suppose it was almost a credit purchase arrangement, but there were no lengthy agreements, and if I'd stopped paying no doubt we'd have lost the suite. We were proud to have it delivered to Number 64 and just as thrilled when it look pride of place in Number 10.

We had sufficient funds left to pay my Parents' decorator whom I had known most of my life. He covered the lounge and dining room ceilings and friezes with anaglypta paper so they could be painted in the future. He also gave Kevin, my husband, some very useful tips which held him in good stead for the houses we've had to tackle during the many moves we've made. Until his arthritic knee started objecting I have to say his work was excellent.

For the next few weeks, we spent as much time as possible at the house. I was getting larger with our first child on the way. With the suggestion that it would avoid a fall I was given the deep skirting boards to paint. My Mother made curtains and when we'd finished the house was transformed. We were very proud of our new home, thinking ourselves lucky that we had such pleasant accommodation.

You may say I'm old and have no idea what it's like nowadays. Life is so hectic; having to go out to work, look after children and a home. But I worked. I kept working until I was 75. With the help of my husband I also brought up a son and daughter. After my Father died we had my Mother living with us for her last eight years and I've no real complaints. The good parents of the day, and there were many of them, including mine – in fact I would say the vast majority, taught us respect for people and property. Those sessions round the table at meal times had us talking about the happenings of the day. In the evenings we listened to the wireless (now called the radio), played cards or other games, read books and twice a week, on Wednesdays and Saturdays we all went to the cinema. After 1942 there were just the three of us, my brother having left to join the army. Sundays were visiting days, with us either going to one of my aunts or them coming to us for tea, bringing their children. I'd play games with my cousins, or, when we were older, go for walks.

Fathers would often be found in the local park playing football, cricket or tennis with their sons whilst Mothers taught daughters to cook, knit and sew. Many reading these words today would find fault, especially in the division of people into classes and the segregation of activities between men and women with the women often restricted to looking after the welfare and comforts of their husbands and children. During my life there have been changes, many for the better, but the continued development of the electronic age seems to me to have heralded a corresponding fall in what we would have called standards. Television stifles discussion between parents and children whilst they silently watch 'the box', eating meals from trays, often hardly tasting what are seldom home cooked recipes. E-mailing and texting distances many from the art of conversation, and weekly family outings to the cinema have been replaced by videos or computer games.

During and just after the Second World War even the poorest of families in those dingy but spotlessly kept terraced houses spent time together. I've often heard tell that, like us, they were happy regardless of the conditions in which they lived and the luxuries beyond their limited means. They experienced a richness impossible to value in monetary terms. I'm no supporter of a class system, nor do I champion the misery and degradation suffered in those times. But I do wonder if the 'poor of today', with their increased financial, electronic and housing comforts are any better off than their predecessors, in real terms.

CHAPTER 2

MILKING LIFE

Door to door

Mr. Wright was the first dairyman I can remember. Long before the start of the Second World War he could be heard entering the bottom end of our Manchester Avenue every morning except Sundays. The two wooden wheels of his push cart, shod in metal, used to groan under the weight of the large churn it carried together with the equipment, including pint and half pint measures used for ladling out the milk.

Rarely did his time of arrival vary and this plus the noise of the cart gave ample opportunity for Mother to be waiting outside our number 19 to receive our daily supply. Many neighbours and some of the older children would run to queue behind the cart but she somehow managed to appear the moment he drew level. She was always armed with the traditional blue and white horizontally striped jug, which, approaching Mr. Wright, she held out whilst he dipped the metal measure into the churn. It was a rounded open vessel, tube shaped for pouring, attached to a long straight handle, curved at the end, and designed for reaching deep into the churn. Somehow he was always able to carefully pour the appropriate quantity with never a drop spilt.

If Mum was out, she would leave her jug on the doorstep. It was covered by one of the lace mats which were all the rage at the time. Crocheted out of thick cotton or wool, matching blue and white beads were sewn into it at regular intervals to hang down over the sides, their weight keeping it in place. Mr. Wright would leave the usual measure, confident the cover would protect it from the birds. In those days only one type of milk could be bought off the cart. If we were to be treated to the luxury of cream, this meant a five minute walk to his dairy to buy a small cardboard carton full.

Payment

Once a week, the milkman made his afternoon round trip to collect his money, usually on a Friday – probably because for many working in the mills and factories, pay-day was Thursday. Our bill was rarely more than three shillings (fifteen pence in today's currency) and I would say that was the house average for the neighbourhood. This meant he needed a large leather bag of change which he supported on a strap across his shoulder. He would swivel the bag round in front of him, give a hefty shake and then dive in to find the correct change.

The currency was quite different in those days. We had big old pennies (it would take twelve of them to equal one old shilling - 5p of our current money). There were small silver coins for three old pence, for six old pence, and twelve pence, plus silver twenty four (a florin) and thirty old pence pieces, the latter being called half a crown. We had bank notes worth ten shillings (equivalent to our 50p pieces, and one pound (equivalent to our current £1 pieces). For those wealthy enough to have them, the Five Pound notes were about three times the size they are now. In our time, they were a rarity and to us Ten pound notes were non-existent.

Payment earned a tick in our milkman's record book which he kept in the large side pocket of his knee length brown overall type coat. People trusted each other, not bothering with receipts, although the cautious ensured he added that tick against their name.

The jug would usually be kept in the coldest part of the house. We didn't have a fridge – no one did. Many had small, square 'larders' with marble slabs, ample ventilation, no windows and wooden doors to keep down the temperature. The rest found the coldest place, often under the stairs, not just for milk but for the pies, meat, and all the other items casually flung into fridges today. Sometimes the milk went sour and then it would most likely be used in baking. It was very good for scones. Not being rationed during the war years, it could also be repeatedly strained through muslin to produce a type of cottage cheese which supplemented the permitted quota.

Mr. Wright continued his daily ritual until, having turned sixty, he admitted to Mother he was finding the effort of pushing his cart too demanding. He'd sold to a Mr. Drabble. Mother said he would be sorely missed and greeted the arrival of his replacement with some apprehension. She needn't have worried. Mr. Drabble was well able to continue the tradition, although he did bow to progress. He duly arrived with his modern transport: a horse and cart.

Top of the milk

The big milk churn disappeared, to be replaced by wooden crates packed with glass bottles. The cart won an extra two wheels, all four were clad with rubber and delivery was to our door without our having to be disturbed. This enabled Mr.

Drabble to start earlier and finish quicker but lost us one focal point for neighbourly greeting and activity. I was already familiar with the bottles, having been compelled to drink the compulsory one third pint during the morning school break. Each bottle was sealed with a cardboard top specially made so a small circular piece could be pressed out of the middle to remove it. If you were too brutal, your finger poked through to collect a coating of cream which had settled on top.

Often we would clean the cardboard disks, keeping dozens of them to thread strands of wool through the small centre holes. We then made them into coloured balls for babies' prams, or dolls with faces sewn on, fastened to our dresses or coats using small gold safety pins. (This was before health and safety intervention, but I never heard of any injuries.) The boys turned them into snakes or weapons and often did the same with used postage stamps cut off envelopes.

Manchester soon became accustomed to the new pint or half pint bottles and members of many households like ours would fight for the chance to take the 'top of the milk' for spreading on our puddings or in coffee - a quick substitute for the cartons of cream. One product labelled 'Camp Coffee', in distinctive square bottles was all the rage, although I doubt if our European Masters would allow us to even call it coffee today.

Most back gardens were large enough to grow some fruit and veg. and Mr. Drabble's horse made a valuable contribution to the neighbourhood. Many a man would be standing at the ready with bucket and shovel to grab what might be deposited from the animal's rear end, and there were sometimes heated arguments over who was entitled to the steaming manurial bounty. It was prized for growing rhubarb, vegetables and first class roses.

So, for some, it was a sad day when horse and cart were replaced by the distinctive whirring of motors as specially constructed four wheeled transport glided the milk down the Avenue. With these vehicles tapping over night into the ever available man made resource of electricity, we began to see less of the dairyman, who would often arrive even earlier in his milk float. Despite the clinking of bottles and the muted sound of the engine, he was more difficult to hear than the rattle of the cart or the horses metal rimmed hooves on the road. Any variation to the daily supply was ordered by leaving a message in an empty bottle.

We still saw our milkman on Friday afternoons when he called to collect his money, still using that heavy leather bag full of change. By then I was mid way through my teens, and only too happy to stand in for Mother if she had to go out shopping or on one of her war time activities. He was young, handsome and welcome over my doorstep any time. He still contributed to the community in other ways as well, offering young lads the opportunity to earn pocket money transporting bottles from float to house and collecting the empties – an early recycling operation. Our man was sorely missed when called up for compulsory military service in the Second World War, by me and a number of other young females in our area.

For most, the daily human contact with our milkman began to disappear with the arrival of horse and cart, then the float. What was a social, neighbourly activity reduced to a straightforward business transaction. Now bottles and wooden crates have disappeared, along with our local dairy, and a vast, impersonal industry has grown to replace that unchilled, unskimmed jug of milk with so-called healthy alternatives. We live in the age of ghostly middlemen, supermarkets, and the cars and fuel we use to reach them, all so we can take what we want off the shelves without having to talk to anyone.

More of us now don't even bother to visit the shelves, ordering by text or phone or internet or something. I suppose this does at least save fuel and the associated pollution, except that the International Food Sellers have invested in vans that can deliver not only milk, but almost anything else we want. Community contact suffers further and I doubt if this door-to-door service will ever replace the horse and cart with our grandchildren – girls as well as boys - earning their pocket money helping collect the 'empties' for recycling. Instead, the world will be hell bent on thinking of much more complex ways of seeking global cooling.

CHAPTER 3

ABANDONED

Holiday 'abroad'

Sunday morning, 3rd September 1939. We were on holiday, staying in Douglas, Isle of Man. I couldn't understand why my parents were so anxious to join other guests huddled around the radio. Apart from newspapers, 'the wireless' as we called it, was the only method of receiving speedy bulletins of what was going on in the world. A voice talked out of the large wooden framed set, volume turned up so all could hear. Mr. Chamberlain, the Prime Minister, was speaking, and, gradually, even at the age of twelve I was able to grasp the importance of the situation. We were at war.

Reactions to the news by those around us that, after only twenty one years, Britain was again fighting the Germans convinced my elder brother and I that things were serious. The holiday atmosphere evaporated as a queue formed to use the hotel's public telephone. Anxious guests waited their turn to feed coins into the slot before pressing button 'A' the moment an operator connected them to schools, officials, friends and relatives on the mainland. Information was shared, and for the first time I heard the word 'evacuation'.

To begin with it didn't mean much, until my parents sealed themselves away with our hosts. Dad and the owner of the small hotel whom we called Uncle George, had been school mates, a friendship both my parents had continued with him and his Wife. I got on well with their eldest daughter Jean, the same age as me. We'd resumed a friendship where we'd left off from a previous visit. I remember us both waiting whilst the closed door discussions took place, then I was taken to one side. To my surprise, I was told I was to stay behind when my parents left the island with my brother. Even then I didn't realise what the decision meant, helped I suppose by the careful way it was put to me.

My father had managed to change tickets for an earlier voyage to Fleetwood – the most direct route, connecting with a simple tram journey to Blackpool and a train direct to our Manchester home. He told me the rest of them – my mother, brother, and he had to return.

"It won't be for ever," he said, "and at least you have friends and will be with a family you know." Two days later, they were gone.

The hotel owner's wife, whom I called Aunty Clarice, took Jean, her younger sister and me shopping after the boat left. I was in a sort of dream which extended through the lunch we had in a local restaurant. Only later did I realise this was to distract me from the departure, helping me begin adaptation to a world of uncertainty which had no obvious end. For the first time I'd been separated from my family, my school friends, my routines and my home. The suddenness of the loss and what it meant slowly began to surface, despite the efforts of my friend and her parents to welcome me into their lives.

I went to Jean's school on the island, joining pupils who wanted to know where I'd come from, what life was like on the mainland, in a big city? They too tried to help, accepting me into their world. My previous convent education enabled me to tackle subjects such as mathematics and English without difficulty. They said I talked 'different' until, after a week or two, almost subconsciously, I slipped into their Manx way of speaking. Despite their efforts, I began to know the true meaning of 'evacuation'. Although deep down I accepted that my parents had done it for my good, it didn't help the feeling of sadness, of abandonment. I became homesick.

In a carefully planned Government Operation thousands of city children were being separated from their parents. Unlike me they were gathered in collecting areas, labelled and transported to safer locations where families were paid to look after them for the duration of the war. Many, like me, were made welcome and some developed ties they maintained for the rest of their lives, but I'm sure they must have had moments of loneliness. Later I heard stories of less favourable treatment which made me realise how lucky I'd been.

Mum and Dad tried to keep in touch, supplementing letters with occasional trips to the phone box outside the post office at home. Apart from the seven minute walk it would have cost them at least two old pence for each call, not a small amount out of Dad's weekly wage of about £3. We were lucky the hotel had its own phone, a rare luxury, but I often wonder whether they saw through my cheerfulness when we spoke, detecting how much they were missed. I was still trying to adjust when one evening, the phone rang. Uncle George answered it. When he returned he smiled at me saying he had good news. Dad was coming over to pick me up. There hadn't been any German bombing over Manchester and my parents felt it was worth risking taking me back.

Coming home

It would be impossible to fully describe my feelings. Even now, thinking back brings tears to my eyes. In those days families meant so much and I'd hated being separated. Suddenly I felt guilty, aware how much my adopted Uncle, Aunt and their children had put themselves out to make me comfortable, but I think they shared my joy, and understood. From that moment I had difficulty controlling my impatience until, on the last Wednesday in November 1939, less than three months after I had been left, my Dad arrived.

We set off the next day. At the harbour, I expected to see one of the ferries, the Lady of Man or the Manx Maid waiting for us. Both had been withdrawn for war work, replaced by what looked like a fairly large fishing boat. It was much smaller than the ferries, and at first I didn't believe we were to sail on her. Just ten passengers boarded to join the crew, and soon we were watching the Island slip away behind us. My Dad took me below deck and gave me a puzzle book to work on. I'd made previous trips without difficulty but somehow this boat seemed to be twisting and turning in the open sea much more than I was used to.

Suddenly, for the first time, I felt seasick. It wasn't until Dad took me on deck that we discovered we were in the middle of a serious storm. A crew member told us the boat was pitching so much he and his mates couldn't help sliding all over the place. It was one of the worst crossings he'd experienced.

The man found us a sheltered spot with a small seat welded to the deck. Clad in the pixie hood and scarf Mum had knitted, with a life jacket tied round my shoulders, I did as Dad told me and tried to keep my eyes on the horizon. The ship tossed up, down and sideways through the waves, but slowly my stomach settled sufficiently for me to do justice to sandwiches and a hot drink, prepared for us at the hotel before we left.

When our friendly sailor checked to see if we were all right Dad asked if we were making good time. Although docking at Liverpool was scheduled for 2.30 p.m. he said there would be a two hour delay. Father commented that even allowing for the bad weather that seemed a long time, but the sailor just shrugged. It was only later we discovered the boat had taken a zig-zag course to avoid a German submarine. Apparently it was searching to attack shipping in the area.

When we docked, we had twenty minutes to catch the 5.15 p.m. Manchester train. Being unfamiliar with Liverpool, especially in the dark, Dad decided to suffer the expense of a taxi from the Pier Head, and we made it. The engine was building up steam when we raced along the station platform, climbed into a carriage and staggered down the corridor until we found a compartment with only two occupants. Dad had time to lift our cases onto the luggage rack and slide the door shut before the guard blew his whistle and we were off into the night. The journey was uneventful; in fact I have difficulty recalling it, so much had happened in the day. I think I only struggled back to reality when I realised we were easing into Manchester Exchange Station. I was coming home.

Making our way along the platform, my Father carrying all but the smallest cases, I couldn't help a pause to breath in the Manchester air, my air. We climbed onto a tram waiting at the terminus, stowing our luggage under the stairs before sitting on the wooden three seater facing so we could keep an eye it. The conductor inserted his card into a metal box stationed alongside the tram, topped by a clock. He twisted a key, hopped on board and rang the bell for the driver to set off. It was like a phantom journey, the tram rumbling along metal rails embedded in tarmac and cobbles, pausing at numerous stops to allow passengers on and off. The gas street lamps were covered, just leaving a faint glimmer of light, and house and shop windows were blacked out. It was such a contrast to the bright lights of the City I had left for our holiday so few week ago.

Reaching our destination we struggled through the gloom to make our way down Park Avenue. When we found Montrose Avenue it had no lamps on at all. Then I saw a chink of light coming from the door of the house on the corner. Billy, our dog, having somehow sensed and warned of our approach, Mum had risked the wrath of the local warden to stand on the step to greet us. I was home.

Whether by luck or judgement and unlike many a family, we all survived the bombing when it came. Looking back, evacuation was my introduction to what became the lesson of war. It was an education many families had to suffer, emphasising that the trauma extended far beyond those fighting on the front line. It affects all walks of life on both sides. I wonder if that message will ever be passed down to those who today preach death and division?

CHAPTER 4

THE BLITZ

The calm

Christmas 1939; no air raids, and no rationing despite Government warnings of both. Like me, many other children who had been hurriedly evacuated from towns and cities, wondering if they would ever see mother or father again, were brought back home. Particularly in the North of England, remote from the Continent and Germany, a lot of parents decided it was safe enough to welcome them in time to enjoy the festive season. I was so glad to be one of the lucky ones, and looked forward eagerly to the big Day.

At that tender age of twelve (and not expected or allowed to be half as grown up as modern day teenagers), I knew nothing of the extra effort Mum and Dad must have made to create a Christmas close to those of earlier years. But, to my elder brother and I, there were differences. The biggest was 'the blackout'. As I'd discovered on my return from the Isle of Man, authority insisted upon curtains lined with enough black material to eliminate even the smallest chink of illumination at night. We had leaded lights but many householders with plain glass windows crisscrossed them with sticky tape to reduce the danger of flying splinters, should a bomb explode nearby. The gas in the street lights remained on low and the Council had topped them with special shades to darken the image from above. All outside electrical decoration and advertisements were prohibited.

The whole thing seemed a bit unreal, yet it somehow brought families closer together. After morning Church and our main Christmas meal at midday, we listened to the King's speech on the 'wireless'. As a radio it was nothing like the modern computer which has now pinched the title. Ours was housed in a big wooden frame with valves almost the size of lamp bulbs. They lit up and gained in temperature before the sound came. Transistors were a thing of the future, although I suppose you could call our old receiver portable, if you could lift it and still find a place convenient to the outside aerial. It ran on a large cubic shaped battery called an 'accumulator' of which we had two. We took one to the shop every week for re-charging.

On that 25th December day in 1939 we also played with our presents, read our annuals, listened to more radio, maybe made jigsaws and generally enjoyed a celebration principally devoted to our own amusement. In that respect it closely followed the customs of previous years which included dipping into a Cadbury's chocolate selection box.

Despite attempts to ignore the threats of attack and keep going through the festive season into the new year, the Government had little difficulty convincing a large percentage of the population that being at war with Germany was going to seriously affect our way of life. Many had memories of the First World War, barely twenty one years before. Life did however return almost to normal after the initial scares and by January 1940 schools which had closed when the children had been evacuated, were reopening. Mine, 'The Hollies', in Fallowfield, Manchester, taught from nine in the mornings until twelve thirty, then sent us home with massive amounts of homework to complete in the afternoons.

On our first day back we were taught 'air raid drill'. The Hollies was a large house in grounds boasting tennis and netball courts; at least two of our teachers lived at "The Oaks" - the Convent next door. We were assembled and shown the re-enforced cellars where we would go if the bombs came. They were under both buildings and we thought it great fun trying to imagine what it would be like all gathered together when it happened, whatever 'it' was likely to be. We still didn't quite believe it would, not really.

Describing how everyone existed is difficult. We all went about each day in the normal way, yet deep down there was that contradictory feeling, even a conviction, that things were set to change. It hung over us like a dark cloud, fuelled by the reports we were receiving.

Although television was a decade away, we had a diet of moving pictures offered during visits to the local Cinemas. There were five within walking distance of our house and we went once or twice a week. 'Pathé News' came on screen before the big film. Although the ten minutes or so consisted of News Bulletins similar to ITV, Sky and BBC, shown in black and white, the pictures told the stories. Commentators were in the background, heard and not often seen, describing scenes by what we now call 'voice-overs'. It was information without frills, sometimes perhaps verging upon propaganda to keep our spirits up. We were told facts, but unlike current twenty first century bulletins, carefully prepared scripts for the 'voice-over' reporters avoided expressing the obvious. There were no so-called personality correspondents on screen to answer some of the daft questions put to the prima-donnas of modern broadcasting.

'Pathé News' was how we saw our soldiers in action. The five day rescue of the British Expeditionary Force and their allies from the beaches of Dunkirk at the end of May was faithfully reproduced. Daily reports in the national newspapers gave more detail, always twenty four or forty eight hours after the event, censored like soldiers letters when coming from the scenes of battles, but avidly read by our parents. All told of the reality of world war.

Then the bombs came, hitting London and the south coast, killing people, the targets getting ever closer to us. There were even one or two false alarms when the sirens blared out in Manchester, but as children we still felt apart from the action... until 4th September 1940, a year after the war began.

Like many others we didn't have one of the 'Anderson' shelters which were gradually appearing in back gardens across the land. That night the sirens warned of the attack, and we wondered if it was another false alarm. We lifted our small but heavy billiard table onto the dining table and huddled underneath. We heard the planes overhead, our artillery men firing at them and some explosions, but nothing on the scale of what was to come. We stayed under the table until the 'all clear' sounded.

Shelter

Accepting that the attack was not to be an isolated event, Father contacted a local builder and the pitched roof of our washhouse was replaced with nine inches of reinforced concrete. Although we had a garage, we didn't have a car so the space was rented out to one of the few who did. That still left room for the garden tools swiftly moved out of what was now our makeshift 'shelter' to give room for bunk beds. Fortunately it already had electric light, a cold water tap and drop down table.

Whilst work on the roof was being completed and the raids continued, we accepted an invitation to join the Jacksons, our neighbours across the road. They had one of the 'Anderson' type corrugated steel structures set up in the back garden. It was lined with benches down each side, their hardness relieved by strategically placed cushions produced by the lady of the house. Illuminated by a temporary light bulb and really too small to accommodate both families, it was nevertheless a welcome protection against the ever increasing raids. No shelter would have withstood a direct hit, but at least we may have survived a nearby explosion which could have demolished our houses. Several rows of dwellings were razed to the ground in another part of the City, killing many occupants.

Being under attack with no means of fighting back was a strange existence. Women had begun to work on the land, replacing men who had gone to war, and the trousers they wore became the fashion. I always kept a pair at the bottom of my bed, ready with a woollen jumper. They could be quickly donned for warmth on the trip across the road and later in our shelter. Mum also kept a flask of drink or hot soup ready for the warning siren. Sometimes raids would come in waves of two or three a night, lasting no more than a couple of hours with us returning to our beds each time the 'all clear' sounded. When our shelter was ready, we didn't bother. On hearing the siren we would move into the washhouse and play cards, or draughts or read until bed. We had enough electric light to see, the hot drinks and sleeping bags.

It was still hard to comprehend that people in our city were being killed. Every time those sirens wailed they were followed by the drone of the bombers flying above. The ground would be shaking with 'ack ack' fire from anti aircraft guns ringing the City, one 'battery' placed a few avenues away from us in a field near the railway line. The window shattering vibration from the guns could be more scary than the thud of bombs exploding, especially as they often started firing before we heard the approaching planes. Although the enemy was allegedly aiming at the canal, railway lines and factories there was no precision. Sometimes grouped explosives were dropped, attached to sticks and were just as likely to hit residential as commercial areas.

After every night of bombing, people would go out in fear of what they would find, saddened at the sight of some of their beloved buildings and monuments reduced to smouldering rubble. My brother would join others to retrieve pieces of metal 'shrapnel' which had fallen from the shells fired at the aircraft, or even pieces of enemy planes brought down by the guns. Norman was a few years older than me, heading for adulthood and it was his preparation for employment which took the family on a journey in December of that year; a journey I will never forget.

Night of terror

With its docks unloading vital supplies from ships braving the passage to and from America, Liverpool was a major target and suffered far worse than we did, but beyond the River Mersey, towns such as Southport, Blackpool and Cleveleys had not sustained any raids. In fact some children had been evacuated there, so with Norman set to take a two day accountancy exam in Southport, Father decided we would all accompany him to make it a mini-break by the sea.

We booked in to a boarding house for bed and breakfast and after his first day of the exam Norman was rewarded by being allowed to select a 'picture' he wanted to see (we called them 'pictures' then, not 'films'). We had our evening meal and walked to the cinema to settle in our seats for the early showing. On the previous night, although Southport had remained safe, Liverpool had been 'hit'. We'd listened to reports on the wireless over breakfast and could see flames on the horizon, but even that did not prepare us for what was to come. When we left the cinema, an air raid warden was waiting. He said the siren had gone fifteen minutes before and that Liverpool was again 'getting it'. We could hear wave after wave of enemy planes flying overhead.

"Keep close to the wall, and, whatever you do, don't use your torch," he told us.

Although Liverpool was twenty miles away, we could see flames lighting up the sky and we heard the constant sound of explosions from the bombs and anti-aircraft guns. As a contrast, everything immediately around us was black, leaving us to feel our way slowly back to our boarding house, wondering if this was the night Southport would have their first attack.

Next day the proprietress told us a land mine had lodged in a tree just a few gardens away but fortunately not exploded. Although the enemy weren't seeking to attack the town, she said, there was always the chance of a returning plane discarding unused explosives, or having been damaged by our coastal guns or in dog fights in the sky, crashing before it reached the coast. The radio reported at least two hundred killed in Liverpool and many injured. The City was to lose thousands more before the raids were over.

My brother finished his last exam by midday on 21st December, and joined us for lunch before we made our way to the railway station. Father discovered that following the bombing and due to cancellations, there were no trains running to Manchester until the 5p.m. 'businessmen's express'.

We managed to find seats and reached our home Exchange Station by 6.45 p.m. On leaving the train we were told the siren had gone ten minutes ago and sure enough, there was the droning of enemy aircraft approaching and the sound of the ack ack guns. Those aircraft engines had such a distinct deliberate note which made their intention unmistakable. It is a sound I will never forget and for a long time afterwards, when the war was over, I still dreaded hearing any similar aircraft noise. I still do.

We were standing in complete darkness on the platform of Manchester's main railway station, aware that tracks and trains were amongst the enemy's main targets. We didn't know if the flashes in the sky were from exploding bombs or the guns, but they seemed to be getting nearer. We struggled to the exit as quickly as possible and found a tram stationary outside with a 'Depot' sign showing. My Father approached the driver and guard who were standing talking and explained we only needed to go to two stops before the Depot.

"Jump on," the guard told us. Helping with the luggage, he ensured we were seated and almost immediately the tram drew away. The raid intensified, rattling the windows as we went, bombs exploding nearby. Beams from searchlights swept across the sky seeking to illuminate the aircraft. We could see the streaks of tracers pumped up by the 'ack ack' at those moving enemy targets. Slowly the night transformed into a bright red glow as more buildings went up in flames and we huddled in our seats mesmerised by the scenes so vividly displayed through the tram windows.

Somehow the tram kept going until, to our relief, it reached our stop. I can still picture us hurrying into our Avenue whilst the raid continued, wondering if, any moment, we would be the next target. Fortunately our district was not hit and we were glad to rush indoors. Guns kept firing and wave after wave of bombers continued to drone overhead whilst our ever practical Mum put the kettle on, made the tea and produced the barmcakes she'd bought in Southport. Buttered and topped with some potted beef paste, they were transported to our shelter where we stayed to sit out the raid. I don't know how long it went on but it seemed like for ever before we heard the 'all clear' siren and could relax.

The following night saw us again huddled in the shelter whilst more raids hit our City. Then, for three days over Christmas, there was a lull. Like many fellow citizens we ventured out to discover the extent of the damage that had been caused. Much of the City Centre had been destroyed, the only saving grace being that with the raids taking place at night when offices and shops were closed, the death toll had been minimal. We saw factories still smouldering and learnt that our docks had been hit as well.

That December attack was not the last. Bombings continued for another eighteen months, until mid 1942, bringing more and more destruction to towns and cities across the land. Even the 'buzz bombs', those unmanned flying torpedoes of death reached as far as our City. They too had a distinctive engine noise but the most frightening thing about them was when the engine stopped. We knew that in the silence that followed they were coming down and could do nothing but await the inevitable explosion. Somehow we adapted our lifestyle, continuing with our daily events but ever ready to plunge for cover when the siren went. We had to be vigilant and were often in fear of our lives but it was that December 1940 journey back from Southport and the following night of raids which brought home to me the reality of war and the death and destruction it caused.

WARTIME LIVING

Rationing

Several weeks before food rationing hit Manchester and the rest of the United Kingdom, people were summoned by government announcement to attend at designated locations. Books containing tickets were issued in stages and, our family name beginning with 'B', my mother was amongst the first to obtain ours from the Town Hall. We had four, one for each of my parents, one held for me and one for my elder brother. Pages were divided into sections, the number '1' printed in each square with the word 'coupon' underneath.

From 8th January 1940 purchase of butter, sugar, and bacon required coupons, and you couldn't just go anywhere to buy. Registration with your chosen grocer was needed first. He had to tell his supplier who had to tell the wholesaler to ensure a reasonable level of stock. He would stamp the book and then, when a purchase was made, one or more of the coupons would be cut out. The individual squares had no perforations which meant application of scissors by the supplier and scrutiny by the customer to ensure no more than the required number were extracted. Petrol rationing was so severe, many car owners mothballed their vehicles for the duration of the war. Sometimes the vehicles were requisitioned for use by the Armed Services. Controls were soon extended to other foodstuffs, plus clothes, materials and household items.

A few basics such as bread, fish, offal, fresh fruit and vegetables escaped control, but were constantly in short supply. Mum tried to be early if she wanted any, for the queues soon formed and stocks ran out. I look at t.v. reports of nations across the world suffering similar difficulties today. In Africa and Asia their plight is much greater but it is strange to realise that, within living memory our Country was faced with the death and deprivation of war. If history is traced back one more generation our poor were hit even harder than in our time. Is it a phase every developing nation has to go through?

When clothes were drawn into the scheme in February 1941, sixty points were allocated to each person for the whole year, reduced after twelve months to 48. Twenty six allowed purchase of a man's suit, whilst a ladies' frock required seven. Silk stockings could be bought with only two, although at a cost of four shillings and eleven pence per pair (25p in modern currency), the wages of the day made them expensive. When I started work I earned One pound ten shillings a week (£1.50), with £1 going to Mother for my keep.

With such limited resources, stockings were saved for special occasions and the first rather unsophisticated fake tan appeared on the market. For many girls even this proved too expensive and they were known to resort to watered down gravy browning as a temporary solution – not a good idea if it started raining. Artificial tanning was restricted to legs and any attempt at male participation would have been ridiculed. Sun machines and beauty parlours were decades ahead.

The Americans

Nylons first featured in 1942 when the USA entered the War. American servicemen began arriving in London during the spring, soon to spread out into the rest of the Country. The nearest group to us, at Burtonwood Airbase, near Warrington, numbered thousands. Before being let loose on the locals each airman was obliged to attend lectures introducing them to English customs. They also received small booklets instructing them upon how to behave and illustrating peculiarities they might encounter. Reproductions of the booklets are still on sale today.

Insufficient residential facilities on the airfield meant that almost every house in Manchester was canvassed by officers seeking spare accommodation as billets for their personnel. Three neighbours in the Avenue had space and took men in. Their paying guests would have brought a couple of pairs of nylon stockings with them, the intention being to give them to the lady of the house. However these, and other pairs which drifted over from the States, often found their way to what were called 'cheap' or 'fast' girls. Having been brought up a Catholic and educated in a convent school I shared the shame felt by many at the manner in which these young women hung around the perimeter of the airbase or the YMCA in Manchester Centre. They were ready to pick up an American at every opportunity, granting their 'favours' in return for the nylons.

Aged fifteen in those days, although working in my first job, at home I was still treated as a child. My friends were similarly placed and it was a shock when, for the first time, we saw the coloured skins of many of the airmen, coupled with news reports upon how badly they were treated in America.

Whilst this won them sympathy there were strong feelings against a white girl going with a coloured soldier. Ignorance and limited contraception facilities produced the inevitable births of 'half-caste' children. The stigma of pregnancy out of marriage was bad enough in those days and it was considered that mixed parentage would only increase the burden on the child.

According to one of the soldiers living in our road, English girls were far less sexually forward than Americans. There was a smouldering resentment shown against the Yanks by English boys on leave from the war front, which on occasion burst into physical violence. American servicemen were paid well compared with ours, some not being hesitant to buy the favours of the girls. I suppose this was inevitable with many finding it hard to face up to life in a foreign land, seeing it as a way to win companionship. They were light heartedly described as 'overpaid, over-sexed and over here'.

We had relatives living in the U.S.A and from Christmas 1940 we received food parcels made up of tins of fruit such as peaches or pears and meat including ham and spam. Apparently servicemen were reporting to families back home in the States that we were starving and I suppose by their standards, we were. The food was most welcome especially as fresh fruit was limited in shops. It was several years after the war before many saw their first banana.

'Dig for Victory' posters appeared as part of the Government's initiative to encourage us to grow our own produce. All over the country people converted gardens – we had proper gardens in those days, front and back – to plant fruit and vegetables. Chickens occupied back yards to supplement the one fresh egg per person per week allowed under rationing (somehow we seemed to get six for our four). Those without a home supply used dried egg as a supplement.

Allotments owned by local councils were in great demand with children of all ages joining parents to enjoy sharing in the cultivation of potatoes, onions, cabbage, carrots and lettuce. We also grew peas and green beans against a trelliswork fence and I learnt from my Father the secret of rotation – potatoes in one plot one year then sprouts the next. The four seasons were of greater importance for, to a large extent, they dictated our menus. Fresh beans and peas were a winter scarcity as was fruit. Home grown raspberries, gooseberries and black currants were favourites not only fresh but made into jams and conserves. A small punnet of strawberries was a rare summer treat, divided equally between the family and graced with cream skimmed off the top of what was then full bodied milk. Pigswill bins appeared at the end of each road to collect left over scraps for recycling as animal food.

Mother was a good customer of the greengrocer, who delivered our sack of potatoes every three months, but she still had to join the queue before 9 a.m., sometimes three deep and several yards long stretching into the street, to stand a chance of two English tomatoes or, even rarer, three oranges. We were dependant upon supply ships braving the Atlantic Ocean for much of our food. Even with naval protection they were vulnerable to attack especially from German submarines.

Volunteering

The Women's Voluntary Service was a prime mover in the organisation of children into country expeditions to gather blackberries, crab apples, mushrooms and dandelion leaves.

They also collected rose hips to turn into syrup, a valuable source of vitamin C given to children. Members of other groups including the Women's Institute and Red Cross gathered in halls and each other's homes to knit navy, air force blue or khaki socks out of government supplied wool for our Servicemen. In addition they used thick oily wool to knit special fishermen's stockings, handling large wooden needles and wrestling with the weight when they neared the top of the leg. My mother was a member of the Red Cross and many of my friends did as I did, knitting socks on four size thirteen needles. The wool was very thin, and the socks grew ever so slowly, but we persevered with our contribution to the 'war effort'.

It was a time when people accepted sacrifice and helped each other. Clothes were collected for sorting by the organisations, then distributed to victims bombed out of their homes who had lost all their belongings. Wool was unravelled from old sweaters and jumpers, knitted into squares which were then collected to be made into blankets. Other garments were cut up for stitching into patchwork quilts with the left overs used for dusters and rags. It was a time of improvisation with little going to waste. Newspapers were used for a variety of purposes including wrapping up apples to be kept in a dark place, preserved for eating fresh or in pies long out of season.

With coal rationed, I can remember occasions when there were only a few pieces left in the coal shed. Paper was screwed up to light fires or made into harder lumps, wrapped around potato peelings to burn longer, backed up with the 'slack' as it was called – the small bits of coal and dust left at the bottom of the pile. Whenever possible my parents obtained wood and a log fire was a treat to be looked forward to. Few had central heating and many possessed only rudimentary hot water systems.

Moston Colliery on the North side of Manchester was surrounded by one of the poorest districts. Men and boys built hand carts from orange boxes, using wheels found on the tip or adapted an old pram to collect pieces of coal that had dropped off lorries leaving the colliery. There was always some spillage when they were being loaded and in addition, miners had a traditional right to search the spoil heaps and make use of what they could find.

Shortage of food and materials inevitably led to black market activity. Racketeers materialised selling anything that was in demand, often concentrating their activities on the public houses. Rationed goods fetched high prices with the men doing good business. They were almost always men, and their customers were equally male because 'decent' women were not expected to frequent the pubs. Those brave or brazen enough to venture forth were taken to the 'saloon', not the public bar and when they did so in the poorest areas, their children could be seen sitting on the steps outside awaiting one or both parents. The racketeers tended to wear rather striking clothes which, combined with a distinctive self confident attitude earned them the nickname 'spivs', a title still used today.

Rationing continued after the ending of the war for a further nine years. Victory was no guarantee of instant recovery and the effects of death and deprivation lingered into the next decade. Even so, in our centrally heated, double glazed, world of plenty, it is difficult to re-live a time of threat when recycling, conservation and rationing was a way of life, not just a vague council target.

CHAPTER 6

EMPLOYMENT

An early start

Ages twelve to eighteen are amongst the most important in any child's life. Growing through them as I did between the 1939 and 1945 world war, guaranteed even greater impact. Children remained children. They weren't sent down the mines, and they didn't have the threat of drugs or need of 'ASBOS'. They obeyed parents and teachers, and showed respect for elders. In the main, they were loved. I certainly was.

Cheekiness or rude behaviour would quite likely earn a smack on an arm or leg; disobedience resulted in what is now called 'grounding' - being sent to the bedroom or prevented from joining pals to play. It didn't break spirits or arrest development, but especially if the punishment threatened food time, it encouraged the art of apology. During and after the war years, we were expected and indeed enjoyed family meals round the table.

Looking back, the U.K. educational system of the time seemed simple compared with the current ever changing experiments and organised confusion. Pupils attending Elementary Schools could leave at fourteen to visit what is now the 'Job Centre' with their parent. There were enough offers of employment to start their experience of adult life. Those at Grammar or High Schools were expected to stay until fifteen to sit their 'School Certificate Exam', with potential University applicants entering the Sixth Form to gain the 'Higher School Certificate'.

Greater emphasis was placed upon practical training. Apprenticeships saw entrants working under skilled guidance on the factory floor or within the various trades. Those seeking to enter the professions such as law or accountancy were similarly subjected to years of office activity. The period in the armed forces was often postponed whilst students completed their training, an exemption continued into the nineteen fifties, whilst compulsory 'National Service' remained. With or without university qualifications, most young girls and boys had a grounding which involved dealing with every day people and consequently with community life before they could call themselves fully trained or qualified.

I left school in 1941 when I was fourteen. Pinned on the notice board were details of a scholarship to the Gregg Business College. It was my ambition to become a shorthand typist, perhaps influenced by my Father's employment in a solicitors' office. With the closing date just a week away my parents agreed I could try for it.. My school headmistress reluctantly allowed me to sit the entrance exam and was amazed when I passed. So began my introduction into the Manchester business world, studying shorthand, typing and book-keeping.

Three quarters of the £20 fee for the one year course was paid by the scholarship, my parents having to find the rest (nearly one month of my Father's pay). The school was in the centre of the City on the opposite side of the street to the Y.M.C.A., a mecca for many of the young American Servicemen stationed in this country. Occasionally we would get visits from one or two of them interested in comparing our shorthand techniques with those they'd learnt. Although 'Pitmans' was the favoured style in England, the American version called 'Gregg', which we were taught, was beginning to grow in popularity.

One young man in particular spent time with us. He demonstrated his skill, covering the blackboard at a terrific rate, earning our admiration. Years later I realised that he saw it as a means of overcoming his loneliness in a foreign country, no doubt happy to demonstrate something he'd learnt at home.

First job

I gained my Royal Society of Arts certificate in all three subjects and was nearing the end of the course when the Secretary to the Headmistress announced she was off to join the Women's Auxiliary Air Force. I was offered her job and duly commenced employment at the age of fifteen. The weekly pay was One pound fifty pence, with responsibilities covering stationery buying, collecting money for its sale to students, receiving the tuition fees, and balancing the petty cash. I handled the headmistress' correspondence with the job also requiring me, on two nights a week, to teach school shorthand classes.

Like so many others, responsibility was placed upon me at an early age, reflecting the shrinking work force as more and more were 'called up' to fight in the war. From being school children at fourteen, we were suddenly in the midst of industry, commerce and the trades, coping with the freedom of earning our first pay whilst still under parental control. Looking back, the transition worked. Girls like me started as junior office staff, moving on to more senior secretarial jobs often within the same firm. Others became trainee hairdressers whilst some took shop assistant and waitress posts, many until they were old enough to study as nurses. But believe me, that parental control was much more than a token gesture. Even during the first years of our working lives, we still had to have permission for a night out and had to be in by a set time.

After five months at my first job, I became ill. Diagnosed as anaemic, the Doctor suggested the responsibility shouldered at such an early age, combined with lack of sleep during the bombing raids, was the cause. Although the symptoms eased I eventually told Miss Dix, the headmistress, I would have to resign. She did her best to help, arranging an interview for me with J.D.Morrison & Co. Ltd. They were agents for manufacturers such as Wharfdale Wireless, Guest Keen and Nettlefolds, Roberts Radio and handled the first company in England to market p.v.c. coated wires. My interview was with a dour Scotsman.

"You're too young for the job," he declared. "Besides, according to the college, you've been earning more than I have a mind to pay. How much was it?" I confirmed it was One pound ten shillings a week (£1.50).

"I was thinking more of One pound five shillings (£1.25), but I've agreed with Miss Dix to match what you've been getting. She says you're worth it and I hope she's right."

That was it. I was employed and was taken to meet the Company Secretary, a pleasant lady of what was to me the ancient age of thirty two. She and I were the only internal staff, apart from the storekeeper and the boss. Four sales representatives travelled the Country (in those days called 'commercial travellers'). I discovered how old she was later when describing her to my Mother. They were both attending the same first aid classes.

Job number two

The start of my new employment was not a smooth one. Within a few weeks I developed a swelling called a wicklow under the nail of the third finger of my right hand. It was very painful. It meant no shorthand or typing for three weeks. The treatment then was to protect the finger with a 'finger stall' whilst the nail came away. For some strange reason I was ambidextrous, which saved me. I was able to write up filing cards with my left hand and add up columns in the cash books. Computers had yet to take over and adding machines were only just making a general appearance.

I also did the errands to the post office and helped out where I could. The staff were sympathetic but neither would it have occurred to me or been accepted by them that a trip to the doctor would have resulted in a note earning time off. We all got on with things and I believe were the better for it. Anyway a sick note would have cost money at the time and you needed to be really ill to request one.

My problems were nothing compared to the difficulties of my elder brother. Called up to join the Royal Army Service Corps, he suddenly suffered two blackouts after surviving a bombing raid and machine gun attack in the Isle of Wight. The second was whilst driving a lorry and he landed in a ditch. After a medical check-up, he was transferred to the Royal Army Pay Corps in recognition of his accountancy training. With his new Headquarters only a twenty minute bus ride away, he was billeted at home. During time off he met a girl on one of his trips to the local Palais de Dance. She lived five miles away and after seeing her home he often missed the last bus.

One fateful night he was again facing the walk, this time in a rainstorm. Whether it was just his foolishness, or whether there was a link to his earlier trouble are matters for speculation. Whatever the reason, he ended up in Crumpsall Hospital with pleurisy, an inflammation of the lung and chest cavity membranes. In those days it was a serious life threatening condition, the cause often being difficult to trace. Towards the end of an eighteen week period, demand for beds was increasing with the return of seriously wounded soldiers and he was moved to a Unit on the edge of Delamere Forest. Known locally as Delamere Sanatorium its official title was The Crossley Sanatorium.

Current health problems

It was an isolation unit. That meant extra precautions were taken to guard against the spread of infectious disease. My brother shared a room with a twenty five year old former policeman suffering with tuberculosis (referred to as TB). They became firm friends, helping each other to survive in a world apart from normal people.

At the time TB was a mysterious air born disease which invaded the lungs. No one quite knew where it came from or how it was carried from person to person. Nurses and doctors wore masks but were still in danger of infection from patients, especially when particles of their saliva entered the atmosphere whilst they coughed or fought for breath. Chance of survival seemed more akin to a lottery than to scientific advancement.

It is difficult now to appreciate how primitive were the methods used during those second world war years and indeed into the nineteen fifties. Antibiotics had not been developed. Treatment for serious lung disorders was principally based on fresh air. This meant that in the room the two men shared, the full length glazed double doors to the garden were opened as far back as they could go, every day. Patients were encouraged to breath as much fresh air as they could, sometimes even when, during winter months, snow blew in. I shudder at the reports of South Africa's millions fighting a similar threat today, where what is known as XDR-TB, a drug resistant variety is reaching epidemic proportions. Are we witnessing another black death invasion to rival AIDS?

My brother spent eighteen months in the sanatorium before he was pronounced fit to return to civilisation. During that time he had to have fluid drawn off his lungs on a regular basis and was in frequent pain whilst he fought for breath. Fortunately his condition improved. Unfortunately his friend the policeman was not so lucky. Like so many others, he died before my brother was released.

Norman's army career was over. In addition he was also told that for at least two years he must be out and about. A static desk job was not an option, which put paid to his accountancy ambitions. Fortunately, with so many called up to fight the war, he was able to obtain the type of employment that suited his condition. Leather was in great demand, and the job he took was as an agent to a wholesale supplier. It wasn't a question of selling. There was a ready market, so it was more a question of organising supplies and complying with Government restrictions.

He arranged delivery of the treated skins as well as the punches, special knives, and glues. With many of the larger firms taken over to manufacture ammunition, smaller concerns and even individuals developed the art of cutting the treated leather into basic patterns before holes punched along the edges were bound together with thong (thin threads of leather) to make the handbags, purses, wallets, brief cases, lamp shades and the like. With demand outstripping supply there was a thriving black market, many families struggling to supplement incomes depleted whilst their men-folk were away fighting. They risked penalties if they were discovered.

My Father's job in a solicitors' office gave him access to very old deeds which were often ceasing to be of legal documentation value. They were made of skin and heavily waxed. With the permission of his bosses, he was able to take some of them home and my brother supplemented his income by converting them into lamp shades. He was artistic and they became popular with his clients.

Food was short and incomes meagre, but after the weekly payment of £1 went to my parents for my upkeep, there was still enough for my friends and I to enjoy ourselves. A seat at the cinema cost three old pence and a posh one six pence (2 ½ p), with two old pence for a bag of chips on the way home.

Adversity seems to bring out the best in people and that was certainly my experience of life as a teenager during the Second World War. We appreciated what we had. We improvised to enjoy entertainment as a family. That slogan 'Make do and mend' was frequently repeated, covering all sorts including dresses past their best being cut to make clothes for children. The left over wool from those old sweaters unravelled to provide blanket squares and jumpers was used for hats, gloves, socks and more. Families worked, rested and played together, and shared the life of their community. That was our enjoyment, probably our salvation with so much death and destruction around us.

MY BROTHER, NORMAN AND I AGED 20. HE WAS 25 AND INVALIDED OUT OF THE ARMY

MY SISTER-IN-LAW ON RIGHT WITH ME SHOWING 'THE NEW LOOK'.

1949 – BRIDESMAID AT MY BROTHER'S QUIET WEDDING TO IRENE.

ME AND MY FRIEND MARGARET ON RIGHT AT 17 (1944)

ME ON LEFT WITH MARGARET ON HOLIDAY AGED 16

CHAPTER 7

ENTERTAINING

Leisure activities

In Manchester during the Second World War, we lived a different life. Many Dance Halls and Theatres closed shortly after the outbreak of hostilities and didn't reopen until after the worst of the bombing was over. The cinemas were more determined. With television still in the future, they offered the only moving pictures of the world.

There was a great choice of venues – the Regal, Grand, Palace, Arcadia and Kingsway were within walking distance of our house. I usually went twice a week, to begin with accompanied by one or both my parents. When I turned fifteen I was allowed to go with my friends, provided it was for Saturday Matinees, or the first evening showing (called the First House), which started at five thirty. We were out by eight o'clock and I had to be home by eight thirty.

The Arcadia was known as the 'flea pit' and once I recall my head itching all through the programme. When I got home my Mother searched my scalp with the 'tooth comb' to see if I had any unwelcome visitors such as lice or, indeed fleas. I hadn't, and to suggest that the somewhat dingy and cramped environment of the cinema was responsible, was probably grossly unfair – especially as I developed chickenpox within four days. The seats at the front in the Arcadia were three old pence each (about one and a half a penny in today's money). The cost doubled from a point where the floor sloped upwards towards the back, enabling a better view over the heads in front.

The Regal was the biggest Picture House of the five, having been completed just before the start of the war. Seats were much better upholstered, costing six old pence for the stalls and one whole shilling (a modern five pence) for the circle. Monday and Wednesday matinees were at half price. Unlike the others, the Regal seats could be booked for Saturday night showings, saving the otherwise inevitable queues.

Whichever cinema we chose, the programme schedule was the same. First a short film after which came a Mickey Mouse, Tom and Jerry or Popeye cartoon. There followed an interval when the lights came up to reveal usherettes walking down the aisles with a tray of ice cream. One member of our family always joined the queue to purchase us each a small round cardboard carton of ice cream. Why everyone had to crowd round her in all of a rush was uncertain for, before the lights were dimmed again she always came slowly back up the steps ready to sell on the way.

A small flat wooden 'spoon' was supplied with each carton to dig into the ice cream as it slowly lost its hardened texture. It was always vanilla and there were no alternatives, until choc ices arrived towards the end of the war. They were small blocks of vanilla, coated with a very thin layer of chocolate, wrapped in a type of silver paper which seemed to have a greaseproof lining.

Next was Pathé News and then the main feature. Each performance ended with 'God Save the King' - the National Anthem, and we were expected to stand whilst it played. Anyone trying to leave before the final note was frowned upon, to say the least. It rarely happened, for King George VI and Queen Elizabeth were greatly admired for their unending tours of bombed areas. They did much to raise the morale of the injured being treated in hospitals and those who, having lost their homes and most of their belongings, were living in church halls until alternative accommodation could be found for them.

The cinemas afforded a varied diet of make-believe whilst also allowing us to keep up with information from at home and abroad. The reports were usually a day or two behind the newspapers, especially foreign reports, there being no instant fax or e-mail transmissions. 'Pathé News' had also to be developed onto reels of film for transportation throughout the country to the numerous outlets.

Whatever the venue, the evening's entertainment was always rounded off with the bag of chips, purchased from the local shop. A measured portion was shovelled into a small grease-proof bag, with salt and vinegar added, unless you didn't want it and said so in time. Each order was wrapped in newspaper, and we always claimed the chips tasted best from newspapers. We often enjoyed our meals on the walk home.

D.I.Y amusement

Families seemed more adept at amusing themselves. Many evenings would be spent playing card games such as rummy, Newmarket, knockout whist, dominoes, or board games such as snakes and ladders or the new Monopoly. My brother also taught me to play 'shove halfpenny'. We didn't have a special board and equipment, using cotton reels for goals and normal coins. The ruler featured in another indoor game – cricket. It was the bat, with a marble for the ball and a matchbox for the wicket.

At the beginning of the war, there were ten boys and girls in our Avenue aged between eleven and seventeen. The Government had adopted double summer time, which meant extending daylight two hours into the evening - past the bed times for most of us. We had some good summers as well and after tea we would often gather to vote upon which game to play. We usually divided into two teams and it could be rounders or cricket. Often three or four of our fathers joined in, ostensibly to secure 'fair play'. The Avenue was quiet enough in those days to ensure a virtually uninterrupted match.

Another of our joint activities could be described as a variation between 'hide and seek' and street orienteering. One team would count to twenty while the other disappeared. The chasing team would then divide up to catch the others whilst they tried to get back to base undetected.

Now and then my Father would book a tennis court in Errwood Park. He taught my friend and I to play and when we were older we used to go on our own. Although we were forced to concede that we were nowhere near Wimbledon standard, we did develop enough skill to aim a ball or two into the next court - a sure way of meeting the boys.

My mother was a frequent Saturday night host to pals of my brother. He was still in the army, and his friends on weekend leave, who were not so lucky to be billeted close to home, would often turn up. Mum's 'potato pancakes' were a favourite, new to many visitors and popular with us because the main ingredient wasn't rationed. She'd inherited the recipe from grandmother, who had been born in Germany and spent time in London as cook to a high class family. They're called 'rosties' today (probably not quite the same and totally different from potato cakes which are made out of cooked mashed potato – not raw grated potato).

We did have the radio, which as I've already said, we called 'the wireless' - the large piece of furniture with valves the size of light bulbs hidden in the back, and the accumulator which needed charging (pg. 31). Often I accompanied my father on the ten minute trip to the electrical shop. Dennis Black, the proprietor's son, who helped in the shop, was rather dishy, and for me it was a bad day when he reached eighteen and joined the navy.

Dials at the front of the radio controlled volume and station selection, searched by turning a long thin needle in an arc over a list which included a number of foreign stations. Before the start of the war, we could receive Radio Luxembourg on 'Long Wave'. There was a large decorative area on our wireless, incorporating a rigid material through which the sound penetrated. We needed an aerial mounted high up on the outside wall to achieve reception, especially any signals from abroad which were often interrupted. The cable travelled down and into the room via the bottom of the window frame, running along the skirting board to where the set was positioned. Portability was out of the question. After the war, we again tuned in to Radio Luxembourg, this station being my first experience of the top twenty popular records. Broadcast at 7 p.m. every Sunday night it was compulsory teenage listening and for quite a few parents too.

At the start of hostilities I was still young enough to listen to children's hour, but was also allowed to stay up for the later programmes. We all enjoyed the weekly 'It's That Man Again', known as ' ITMA'. Tommy Handley led the cast in what we would now call situation comedy, with various characters identified by their accents and catch phrases. 'Round the Horne' with Kenneth Horne and Richard 'Stinker' Murdock was another half hour regular whilst Jimmy Edwards, Arthur Askey and others also had slots. Most performed live in front of the microphone, the broadcasts going out without delay.

News bulletins were listened to intently to gain as much information of the battles as censoring allowed. They were read in what was then BBC English without any regional accents. Usually we were given the bare facts, it being left to the newspapers to fill in the details. The BBC had no rivals but seemed capable of maintaining impartiality where necessary and, I believe, achieving high standards modern broadcasters struggle to emulate. Competition doesn't always improve standards.

When Dance Halls and Theatres re-opened, my elder brother and his friends, when on leave, would go to the local Levenshulme Palais. Although I'd been working for over a year, my friend and I were not allowed to go until we reached the age of seventeen. Our parents did let us attend the local 'hops'. These evenings were run by Churches of all denominations, refreshments being included in the ticket price. Many were in small halls, using a gramophone for the music. Electrical equipment was replacing the clockwork wind up machines of infant years, but they were only capable of taking one record at a time. The larger halls sometimes engaged a three or four piece local band.

It was at the time I started going to the hops that I noticed boys. Suddenly film stars and singers began fading into the background. Aged between thirteen and fourteen, I was still at school. We all had our own desks with lift up lids, and despite the declining interest our favourite male film stars remained pinned to the underside. Taken from the weekly magazine 'Picturegoer', they were on foolscap sheets (just a bit bigger than the current A4 size), and had to be ripped out - there were no photocopiers. Like most of the others, mine was a changing scene as I shifted my favours from Griffith Jones to Lew Ayres, Franchot Tone and many others.

One of my best friends was like a honey pot to boys. Two in particular, from St. Bede's College, two miles up the road, were usually waiting with their bicycles at the bus stop by the time we got there. Both were smitten by Margot, whilst all I could do was worship from afar - especially the fair one called Arthur Mills. I thought that as I wore glasses, I wouldn't stand a chance. Who would believe that five years' later I'd meet him at a dance, agree to go on a date with him and find him so boring both in conversation and kissing that each time we encountered afterwards I gently avoided his overtures. It shows how our taste in men can change when we reach our twenties.

Allowed out

I remember quite vividly the first time my friend Margaret and I were allowed to go to the Levenshulme Palais. Although we'd heard a lot about it, nothing could prepare us for the contrast from the local halls we'd been used to. It was only ten minutes' walk from home, and, very politely, my Father instructed us to be back by 10.30 p.m. Margaret was to spend the night with us.

In the foyer, we passed inspection by a very large, imposing man before being allowed through the inner entry doors. We could see the wooden dance floor from the entrance hall. It was lined on two sides by tables and chairs with the Band on the raised dais at the top. We could hear them playing as we entered the cloakroom, anxious to change into our silver or gold, strapped dance shoes as quickly as we could, but at the same time pausing just to drink in the atmosphere.

Having secreted our cloakroom tickets for our coats and outdoor shoes (which we stowed in zipped up leather bags we used to transport our dance shoes) in small evening bags made of silver, gold, black taffeta or soft leather if we could get it, we were ready.

Taking a deep breath we entered through the cloakroom door. There was the Bill Edge Orchestra, nine or ten of them well into one of the popular tunes of the time. The line up included piano, drums, sax, trombone, trumpet, clarinet and also a female 'crooner' who was singing a duet with one of the band members. We joined the girls and boys standing at the back hoping to get partners, whilst those already with partners took advantage of the tables and chairs ranged around the room. To us it was so big... gigantic. The dance floor alone was bigger than most of the church halls we'd been used to.

Behind the band there was a cafe selling non-alcoholic drinks, tea or coffee served with, if we could afford them and until the caterers' rationing allowance ran out, sausage rolls, or scones and biscuits. Sometimes, as a special treat, we'd have a finger of slab cake. In the twenty minute interval, many of the boys boycotted the cafe in favour of a visit to the Midway Public

House a few doors away. They were given a 'pass out' for what they called a 'real drink'.

The few women who followed were relegated to the 'saloon', and would only venture there with a male escort if they wished to preserve their reputation. The main bar was strictly for men. Fortunately the dancers' passes expired after forty five minutes, which usually guaranteed their return in a reasonable state.

When one dance ended and the next began, a boy would make a bee line for the girl of his choice. There were never enough boys and the pretty and attractive girls were first choice. In our initial few weeks my friend and I often danced together, a not unusual occurrence. Even with a sprinkling of those on leave, identified by their uniforms, there was always a shortage due to the absence of men called away to war. The specially constructed 'sprung' dance floor was such a pleasure after the solid boards of church halls: we were hardly off it.

Soon we began to be recognised by the regulars until eventually we were seldom without a male partner. Nineteen forties music was much influenced by Glen Miller favourites including American Patrol, In the Mood, Pennsylvania 65000, String of Pearls and Moonlight Serenade. There wasn't an evening without several of them receiving an airing. Then there were the compositions by Irvine Berlin and Rodgers and Hart, taken from the American film musicals. There were English pieces as well, many made popular by Vera Lynn, christened the 'Forces Sweetheart' for her entertainment of our troops.

Usually three tunes were played one after the other with a brief pause between for the band members to change their music. Then there was a pause to allow a change of partners. The repertoire covered quickstep, foxtrot (my favourite), waltz, tango and rumba. Jiving and jitterbugging arrived with American servicemen during the war. Some dance halls had modern and old time nights which were very popular. Favourites including Moonlight Saunter, St. Bernard's Waltz, the Military two-step and the Palais Glide really brought the dancers together. Often they were selected to celebrate someone enjoying a birthday and were great fun.

Compared with the modern smooching around in the clubs and discos, deafened by a beat which destroys any chance of appreciating the music, it was a time of skill and application. There was also ample opportunity for a conversation between dances, which did wonders for the creation of new relationships. Ballroom dancing schools thrived, although my Dad, emphasising the exercise value of learning to glide and move swiftly over the floor, taught me when I was about ten. Just before the war started we went to Blackpool for the weekend. I was introduced to the Tower Ballroom, which has overcome fire and famine - in music and financial terms - to survive as a current mecca for dancing. It hosts numerous competitions, and recent TV coverage of the art - for it is an art - has sparked the revival of an activity which, over the years, has refused to die.

Watching the various celebrities on television losing weight and desperately trying to perform steps which came naturally to us in those post second world war years, brings it all back. My weight never topped seven stone four pounds during my teenage years and I believe my dancing, probably assisted by a diet enforced by rationing and the lack of personalised transport produced a level of health that has benefitted me to the present day.

Dancing inevitably led to other leisure activities. One for me followed an invitation to join a group who regularly met on Sundays to go hiking. Despite the rationing, the blackouts, the shortages, and the bombing, life for teenagers between 1939 and 1945 had a lot going for it. The weekend group thought nothing of hopping on a train from our local Levenshulme station to enjoy a jaunt across the Derbyshire moors. England seemed a nicer place to live, possibly with adversity bringing out the best in people.

Women, including mothers, under the age of fifty, had to take up war jobs, but they still cooked wholesome meals from the rations we received. Many like mine sacrificed luxury items such as chocolates and oranges so that we could have treats. I've already mentioned one popular phrase - 'make do and mend' with old dresses cut up and converted into different clothes, especially for the children. Jumpers and cardigans beyond rescue in their original form were unravelled into skeins, then dipped into warm water to straighten out the wool. Once dried they were rolled into balls so the wool could be used for knitting into other garments. Jumble sales were also very popular. I never heard my Mother or Father moan, they had too much to do. If a neighbour or relative needed any help they were always there, and this was reciprocated in our times of need.

With no T.V. or computer games, children used their imagination to invent new activities. They appreciated trips to the cinema as treats. Reading was popular with libraries often used as a prime method of teaching. In addition to the public facilities, after the war, firms like W.H.Smith ran an active commercial book lending service as, for popular fiction, did our local newspaper shop.

My mother took on part-time shifts in the local library, helping replace employees who had been called up to fight for their Country. She was trained by the head librarian who became a family friend. New books were in very limited supply due to the shortage of paper, and her job meant that we were kept informed of issue dates. We still had to go on the list and await our turn, but it enabled me to read a lot. We all had our favourite authors. Mine were historical or doctor romances, westerns and thrillers. Parents and teachers were respected and often it was a joint effort that ensured sons and daughters were fully qualified readers by the age of six. Manchester also had and still has a famous Reference Library, and I suspect that despite the explosion of the Internet, many a student still uses it as they did in my early days, to assist their exam studies. (I'm told that starting in 2010, half the stock is to be moved into a nearby building with the other one million or so books stored in redundant salt mines during a three year renovation period.)

Public 'baths' were also centres of community activities. There were sections in which those without good home conditions could have a wash and shave in a morning, but our family used them for swimming. Every Sunday morning after attending the 8 a.m. Catholic mass we would meet with my uncle and two cousins to join in the mixed bathing at Levenshulme Baths.

The word 'Entertainment' seems today to demand someone else providing it. In my youth we were used to entertaining ourselves and sharing the activities with others around us. And yes it did include cooking, knitting, and a lot of other pursuits which are now regarded as chores, unloaded whenever possible whilst we sit back in our so called 'civilised' countries and, comparatively speaking, do nothing.

CHAPTER 8

FASHION

Dressmaking

If family history is to be believed, my Grandfather on my mother's side, of Austrian birth, was a colourful character. He followed his elder brother into the army, but having absconded, had to be bought out to avoid prison. He swiftly made his way to England, established himself as a tailor and, rumour has it, his creations included a smoking jacket for Edward VII. He certainly worked for the firm making robes for Queen Victoria's celebration of sixty years on the throne. My mother followed in his footsteps – not the army or to prison but as a qualified tailoress.

She maintained her skill after marrying and setting up home with my Father in Manchester. Leading up to the Second World War she could be seen during the January and Autumn sales buying cloth. Yes, we had sales. Shops were closed on New Year's Day and the rush started on the 2nd January, not before. The same applied in Mid July, but that was it - none of the modern twos for ones, threes for twos, special reductions and other money grabbing all year confusions in between: well not in my Manchester. Sales always finished in a uniform manner. By the end of January stores were concentrating on summer fashions and in Mid-August they were coping with the school shoes and clothes for the new term. At least those routines haven't changed.

My Mother hunted for remnants which were ends of rolls or bales of various materials used to make coats, dresses, curtains and more. There was satin, cotton, silk, taffeta, wool, velvet and velveteen (nylon and polyester had yet to be invented). Whatever was left from the rest of the half year's trading in the major 'in-house' departments of the big Manchester stores was there. Bargain hunters descended on large counters supporting piles of folded cloth. Lengths varied from one to four or five yards of thirty six inch wide material with some other smaller pieces thrown in. A label giving the price was stitched to the corner of each one, all being genuine 'end of roll bargains'. Mother ensured that she was always one of the first in Lewis's (a store that has survived until 2010) to sift through what started as very orderly piles, but, despite the efforts of assistants, were soon reduced to chaotic mini-mountains.

This way Mum always had a good stock. She kept it folded in an old pillowcase stored in a large drawer of the even larger free standing double wardrobe in my Parents' bedroom. Purchases were divided into summer or winter weight with the woollen ones separated for coats and warm dresses.

The patterns

Whilst still in Junior School I would look forward to trips with my Mother to Lewis's material department. Being one of the largest Central Manchester Department Stores it had a whole floor devoted to cloth and accompanying haberdashery. We would spend time studying the readily available pattern books covering the latest fashions before buying a selection. Giving the reference numbers we'd noted to the assistant, he or she would find corresponding envelopes containing the actual patterns in one of the filing drawers. (Stores such as John Lewis still have haberdashery departments selling material and patterns in roughly the same way, but they are of a much reduced size.)

At that time Mum made most of my clothes. Using material stored in the wardrobe drawer, dresses had generous hems which she would let down so I had two years wear out of them. Just before World War II started in September 1939, following a routine she'd established virtually from my birth, she selected some lightweight cotton prints and using patterns specifically designed for young girls, made me fourteen dresses with knickers to match. Some were for that fateful summer holiday which ended in my short evacuation.

When she decided I'd grown out of the clothes she would parcel them up and deliver them to my school, St. Roberts Elementary at Longsight. They were then distributed to the poorer children many of whose fathers were unemployed and who lived in what some would call squalid conditions. In those days poor really meant poor (see Chapter 1).

Patterns at the time consisted of several strong sheets of differently shaped blank tissue paper, shiny on one side, folded into envelopes about the current A5 size with a picture of the finished article on the front. Each of the sheets, when laid on the material, came together like a jigsaw. Often my Mum could be found poised over cloth spread on the table with the pattern pieces placed on top. Beforehand she would have held some of them against me to check if any adjustments were necessary.

When making a skirt, coat or jacket in thicker material she would use sharp edged triangular tailors' chalk to draw a white line round the edges of each piece and then cut out the shapes. The resulting pieces of material would be basted together (attached by temporary stitching) to produce a mock up of the finished garment before she settled down to machine it.

Not being able to use the chalk to create the lighter summer clothes, she would separate sleeves, body etc. and often just cut round the paper shapes one by one. On occasion she'd pin the paper to the cloth before cutting, although this was to be avoided, as it tended to reduce the times the same pattern could be used before it began to disintegrate. Often I'd come into the dining room and see the paper weighted down against the material by various knives, forks and spoons she'd taken out of the cutlery drawer. On occasion she wouldn't bother with mass produced designs, cutting her own patterns out of brown paper.

For cutting my Mum used large, very sharp dressmaking scissors (she called them her favourite black handled shears). From time to time when he visited our street pushing his mobile equipment cart, she would allow the travelling knife sharpener to service them, but she always kept a close eye on him to ensure he did it properly. Also she frequently used her tailor's flat iron to hold down the paper whilst she was cutting around it. When she needed the iron for pressing the finished garments, she'd heat it by lighting the methylated spirits in the mini stove specially made for the purpose. (During the war, electric irons were being introduced; steam irons followed much later to rival the use of damp cloths.)

So many others, like my Mum, bought patterns and made clothes to save not just money but during the war, their clothing coupons. None could afford the throw-away society which we seem to be suffering today, and it was not only the same patterns that were used over and over again. Second hand material would be fashioned into new shapes and would be discarded only when on the point of disintegration. News of my Mother's skills quickly spread through our Avenue and we had many a caller seeking guidance as to how they could overcome this problem or correct that fault. It was a time when knowledge and experience were shared, not only in dressmaking but all the other features of everyday life. The phrase 'Do it Yourself' would have been considered an insult. The community did it together. They certainly knew how to re-cycle.

Adapting to war

By the time the War broke out I'd completed my first year at 'The Hollies' Convent in Fallowfield. We had to wear the standard school uniform bought from Barries, the store in Central Manchester recognised as purveyors of the approved clothing for most of the High and Grammar Schools in and around the City. Like many similar outfitters throughout the U.K. their privileged position not only allowed them to maintain an exclusive 'High Class' attitude, but also to keep their prices up.

At the age of twelve, we girls were not as sophisticated as our modern day counterparts. Trousers for women only arrived with their need to work in the factories and, as I've mentioned, our wearing of them was limited to going into air raid shelters during the bombing. Apart from the compulsory school uniform, our dresses were usually cotton or voile for summer (a semi transparent material worn over underskirts and vests) with one or two in georgette or taffeta for best. Woollen took over for winter.

In the summer mine had round or square necks, often with puffed sleeves but sometimes sleeveless. The more complex had two or three layers of frills along the bottom of the skirts, whilst in winter, according with the accepted fashion of the day, I had collars and long sleeves. Ideas changed in my early teens to include sailor and mandarin collars, no doubt following military uniforms.

In addition to sales' times there would be shopping expeditions. When Mum and I thought we'd found a suitable design, she would buy the pattern and two yards of thirty six inch wide material. During the years of rationing, this would take six of our precious coupons and a wait in the store for the transaction to be completed.

The system of payment always fascinated me. The assistant would make out a bill, tear it from her book, take my Mum's £1 or ten shilling note (there were no £1 or 50p coins or credit cards at the time), place it in a metal canister which was then whizzed along cables to disappear above our heads. Four minutes later it was back, caught in a metal basket positioned at the end of the particular cable. Eureka! There inside was the change and receipt.

My school, The Hollies, had winter and summer uniforms. Summer began on 1st May, even though by then we'd struggled through some sweltering April temperatures in our gymslips, long sleeve blouses, ties and stockings (knee length in lower forms and full length, held up by suspenders, after the fourth form). Travelling to and from school, we had to wear brown gabardine coats and velour hats. The hats were also brown, shaped like a poached egg with the only relief being a band just above the brim in parallel red, blue, yellow and green school colours.

For summer, white ankle socks, blazers and panama hats (again showing the school colours) took over and we were allowed to wear 'banana' dresses. These were made of yellow silk poplin with long sleeves, edged with dark brown cuffs and collars with the same coloured material for the belt. We hated them and wondered if our sewing teacher, Mother Barbara, had had a say in their design. Clad in her black habit, she looked as ancient as the dresses although she was probably still to celebrate sixty years, if she ever celebrated anything. She set us a second year task to make a pair of knickers.

We had to copy a pattern ending each leg just above the knee with a frill she taught us to create by 'drawing a thread' followed by blanket stitching along each edge. A double row of stitching was required at the waist through which elastic was to be threaded with a small button attached at one end. The button was for an embroidered hole at the other end... I think that was how it went. Our class weren't the most enthusiastic participants in the scheme with delays building up to an extent where Mother Barbara, in total frustration and with the end of term looming, told us to take our creations home to finish.

I did as instructed. Although I never wore the completed article it provided amusement for my Mum. She was helpless with laughter when she first set eyes on the knickers, declaring that she hadn't seen anything like it since she was a girl. She couldn't wait to share the story with her friends and in the meantime Mother Barbara cruised on her way, oblivious of the sensation she was causing.

April was as hot as ever in my third year at the Hollies and led to a revolution. One day with temperatures soaring, a number of the girls defied the regulation and arrived wearing their summer ankle socks. Nothing was said at first, but at the end of lessons, Mother Monica, the head mistress, called the whole school to assembly. Announcing that it had been observed that many girls had disobeyed the rules, this would not be tolerated. She had discussed the matter with the Reverend Mother and they had come to an agreement. As a result the summer date would be altered to 1st April. What was more, we learned that the following year would see the replacement of the disliked yellow uniform by light brown and white check voile dresses with short sleeves – a big improvement on the 'bananas'.

And so to work – war years and after

I left college to start my first job at fifteen *(See Chapter 6)*, thrilled at last to be able to wear what I wanted. I've always had a thing about shoes and considered beyond tolerance the school regulation one inch heel brown lace-ups or 'bar' creations. Even with a bit of a stretch I've never exceeded 5 foot 3 inches in height. My Mother was still buying my shoes during my mid teens and I always had a tussle with her, driving assistants to distraction by declaring every offering was either too tight or pinching my toes until we got to a pair with at least two inch heels. Throughout my life the love affair with foot apparel has continued, encompassing square and pointed toes, and up to four inch stilettos.

Dad said one day I would regret cramming my feet into some of the fancy footwear I bought, but in spite of some painful moments and an odd ankle injury I kept going regardless

– until I was seventy eight. If it be known, I'm still tempted today.

After the austere years of the War I would save a weekly half a crown (twelve and a half pence) out of my small wage. This was augmented by another shilling darning the holes in my Father's socks – a job my Mother hated. In those days, being made of wool, and with Dad, despite working for solicitors, doing a lot of walking when collecting rents of tenants of the senior partner's Company, they soon wore thin. The mending wool wasn't rationed. New pairs cost coupons and serious money so at three old pence for two we both did well. Anyway I liked being able to help.

Looking back, it's a bit difficult to get things in perspective. History records that the Second World War started in 1939 and ended in 1945. Rationing didn't hit us until 1941 and was one more hardship to be borne out of nations fighting nations. For two years we each had sixty six clothing coupons. Then they went down to 48 and by 1945 they hit a low of 36, with the controls remaining until 1949. That meant we had to plan what we would need for the year. Mum and Dad would often give me some of their coupons.

Getting knitted

Although most of the initial knitting was of socks for the service men fighting to maintain our freedom, rationing led to more general activity, including cardigans and jumpers for each other. Mum and I would study the knitting patterns in the shops or magazines, often choosing lacy ones calling for three or four ply wool. They took less wool and coupons (one coupon for every two ounces) than the double knitting wool, which although knitted at greater speed on larger needles was an extravagance we generally avoided.

Stripes became very popular, allowing the use of balls left over from the other garments or unravelled from discarded ones. Now, ten years or more into the current century I see that stripes are again in fashion - maybe a sign of return to conservation. Who knows, men might start darning holes in their socks next.

Some of us were better knitters than others. Usually it was an occupation practised by women, my mother having taught me from an early age. We also learnt it at school under the heading of 'Needlework' whilst the boys were expected to do 'Woodwork'. One of the girls with whom I worked, was exceptionally good. She entered a competition launched by Paton & Baldwin, then one of the largest producers of knitting wool. It was run by the Lewis's Department Store, and she won second prize.

Her creation was so attractive I bought it off her for One pound ten shillings (£1.50) - more than half my weekly wage at the time. It was in royal blue and lemon using the fair isle design for the body (fair isle was named after the Scottish Island famed for introducing the colourful 'Moorish' patterns alleged to have arrived with survivors of a wrecked Spanish ship). It was irresistible. It had epaulettes and the blouse-like full sleeves were in pure lemon. I had to wait three to four weeks whilst it was displayed in the store before I could claim it.

Mum found a remnant of fine lemon wool material in her drawer. We chose a pattern together and she produced a suit with a wide cape style jacket, turned up sleeves and a slightly gored button-through skirt to go with the jumper. The result was a perfect match for the high fashion at the time. I wore it on many dates with a selection of boy and girl friends and it was often admired.

Needless to say there was no chance of simply going out shopping, seeing a dress, coat or pair of shoes and buying them. Mail Order as it is known today didn't exist and few private homes had telephones. We could only buy what was urgently needed and it was usual to have a best outfit kept for Sundays and special occasions. When items began to get shabby they were relegated to every day wear and more precious coupons used to replenish the best.

For work, Mum kept me supplied with straight skirts, two at a time, often made out of her old suits which had already seen several years' use. Both Mother and I also knitted jumpers to go with them. Summer dresses did two seasons – when I stopped growing they lasted during the warmer months of many more years. Coupons were saved whenever possible for the purchase of material for a couple of the annual replacements.

With my Mum still making most of my clothes, I can remember the thrill of going into a large shop near where we lived for the very first time. It was 1944 and I tried on a selection before deciding upon a dusty pink wool georgette dress with long blouse-like sleeves and a waist band held with a button. It had a collar, revere and buttons to the waist before descending into a full skirt with soft pleats. The special purchase was for the twenty first birthday party of one of my cousins. It did so much for my confidence that I wore it for very many years.

Fashion for the masses

There were fashion designers like Hardy Amies, Norman Hartnell, Victor Stiebel, Digby Morton, and several others. Their creations were way out of our league and we were by no means classed as poor. Aimed at what was still regarded 'the Upper Classes', these men did however become part of the Incorporated Society of London Fashion Designers. To boost moral in 1942 the Society created 34 designs of 'utility' clothing which won the approval of the Government through the Board of Trade. Each had to have minimal cloth usage, with skirts being nineteen inches off the ground and buttons limited to three per garment. Reginald Shipp designed CC41 labels (standing for Clothing Control 1941) and each item had to have one attached.

With the clothing coupons lasting until 1949 I feel we appreciated things more in those days, employing a great deal of ingenuity. Even when they ended we didn't go mad. Ordinary people couldn't afford to. As a fully qualified Royal Society of Arts certified shorthand (120 words per minute) typist (60 words per minute) coupled with a bookkeeping qualification, at fifteen I started on £1.50 per week with a promised annual .25p rise on each birthday. When I was eighteen I could save up for a pair of new shoes, a blouse, silk stockings, a dress or coat. Credit cards didn't exist and shops only accepted cash.

Out of my increased weekly wage packet, apart from the £1 paid to my Mother towards my keep, two shillings and six pence (30p) went on for bus fares. Ten shillings (50p) went on entertainment and other miscellaneous items needed from time to time and the rest was saved towards Christmas and Birthday presents, give or take a few emergencies - some of which my

Father may have called indulgences. Thinking back, I'm not sure whether clothes came under the miscellaneous or indulgent heading, or both. What I do know is that I had to have hard earned cash in my hand before I could go out and buy.

Clothes were always on my birthday and Christmas wish lists... well they would have been if I'd made any. In those days, lists weren't necessary. Aunts and uncles didn't need them. The aunts always did the buying, their choice being between much needed scarves, gloves, pairs of silk stockings, fancy handkerchiefs attractively boxed often with my initial 'K' embroidered on them, jewellery, perfumed talcum powder and soap. Giving and receiving were pleasures rather than obligations and whatever the season or occasion we enjoyed doing rather than having done for us. Because we shared and valued others as much as ourselves, we were able to graciously accept when our turn came, an art which seems to be disappearing in the current age of greed and pure monetary profit. Life was valued more, comfort and survival less guaranteed.

In summer the emphasis would be on light, bright, patterned materials, no doubt to help counteract the effects of war. Once I bought some linen type cloth with a white background. It had two inch bands of yellow along which there were rows of little 'gollies'. This gave an effect of dancing around the skirt when I moved. My Mum made it into a cap sleeve top with a 'V' neck and a full skirt. This was greatly admired by many although such a design would be politically incorrect nowadays.

Evenings

Before the Second World War, formal evening dress was an almost standard requirement for dinner dances. The same applied to formal dinners with even some of the exclusive hotels insisting upon it for normal evening meals. Men had black evening suits, white shirts and bow ties whilst women were expected to wear full length gowns.

The habit was preserved as much as possible into the war years, many women sticking to their pre-war black collections, enhanced by jewellery. My Father had to attend quite a few functions as did my Mother. Husbands and wives were always included so, before the war, having been trained as a 'gents' and ladies' tailoress, she made him a black evening suit. I was too young to take note of the details but he always looked smart in it. I do recall it had wide silk lapels, and was worn over a white shirt with the front stiffened (some were stiffened with starch) and with several fancy vertical tucks below the equally stiff collar and black bow tie.

My first evening dress was from when I was a bridesmaid at my much older cousin's wedding. There were four of us and we wore a different plain colour, each blending with the other whilst at the same time suiting our individual complexions. Mine was blue. Having to hand over seven precious coupons we all made sure our dresses would have further future uses.

I think I went on to wear mine at a Church New Year's Eve dance or something similar before it was cut down to make a day dress. I remember it was a very cold year with plenty of snow. My Mother knitted me a 'spencer' in fine wool and large knitting needles, for me to wear under the dress. It's interesting to note that these types of garments are again in fashion. Mine was without sleeves to go under the evening dress.

The New Look

1947 saw the launch of the 'New Look' by Christian Dior. Slow to take off at first due to the substantial amount of material required for the dresses, Mother, looking ahead, saved her coupons to fit me out for my twenty first the following year.

The event was much more important than it is today. No one could vote until twenty one and eighteen had no special significance, being like other birthdays. Families, even the poorest, would lay on a spread for the twenty first. Dress for the occasion was very important and, often parents would go to the expense of a supper dance.

Fortunately being only Five feet two and a half inches reduced the amount needed, and in the June of that year we both went in search of patterns and material. For the occasion I wore an aquamarine and diamante necklace on a black velvet ribbon. It was one similar to that worn by the then Queen which my Parents had bought me at the massive price of £20. My shoes were tan coloured leather Clarke's Skyliner with three and a half inch heels... maybe even more, which drove my Father mad.

Only after the ending of clothes rationing in 1949 did the clothes trade begin to return to normal. Gradually many of the mills and factories which had made uniforms for our forces resumed their normal work and the large stores in particular began to display more extensive selections. In Manchester we had Lewis's, Pauldens, Affleck & Brown, Henrys, and Marks & Spencers. At the other end of the City up-market Marshall & Snelgrove traded from St. Ann's Square, with Kendal Milnes, part of Harrods in Deansgate not a venue for the likes of us middle class mortals.

In 1955 my Father paid for 3 silk velvet dresses for the bridesmaids at my wedding. Made in deep red they each had a shot-silk matching rose taffeta fichu. It rested on the shoulders and then crossed at the front to the waist to fall into a waterfall at the back, changing colour in certain lights. Perhaps I should explain that velvet was a closely woven fabric originally made of silk which was very expensive. It had a thick short pile on one side as opposed to the popular 'velveteen' – a cotton imitation of the real thing.

The dresses were from a Vogue pattern and were produced by a professional dressmaker. Having been a bridesmaid myself five times (disproving the saying 'three times a bridesmaid and never a bride') I wanted something the girls could keep to wear afterwards. Money was still tight and they welcomed being able to remove the fichu to give a sleeveless dress with a properly shaped neckline. Departing from the then fashion of big bouquets, I also gave them velvet muffs to carry each with a spray of white carnations angled across the front. Afterwards they were able to turn the muffs into evening bags which I understand saw years of good use.

Being quite skinny in those days (how skin stretches over the years), I was able to select a traditional, close fitting white silk velvet wedding dress. For some reason, despite my subsequent expansion, I've still got it, and the husband that went with it.

Especially during those post war years I was able to enjoy all the latest fashions, often spending my lunch times touring the shops. Only now, looking back, do I truly appreciate how lucky I was to have had Mother's support. She was not alone in the devotion she and my Dad gave to our family. Many in my age group, growing up in those restricted times, benefitted from Parents who cared. We all learnt to pull together and when faced with shortages or restrictions we coped positively rather than sitting back to moan that 'they' should be doing something about it. We did it and it worked. We also coped with the deaths and injuries resulting from the war and respected those who returned from the battlefield without limbs or with the mental wounds after surviving some of the more lethal Japanese and German prison camps.

Compared with today, we missed out a lot on fashion, or did we? It wasn't handed to us on a plate. We had to go out and get it, be a part of creating it, and that might well have been more satisfying than the aggravations of our current throw away society. Looking back it's difficult to appreciate how things have changed during my life. Travel is much easier, communication swifter and treatment more sophisticated. Whether for work or pleasure I suppose it's only right that dress should move forward too, but I hope we never reach the stage where it becomes impossible to differentiate the post-person from the plumber, the policeperson from the nurse or indeed the man from the woman.

THE NEW LOOK, 1947

CHAPTER 9

APPEARANCE

Hair

Before the start of the 1939-1945 War, Mum had my hair cut in a short bob with a straight fringe across the forehead. Later I was allowed to grow the fringe and take it over to one side, held back by a fancy ribbon tied in a bow. The style always looked neat, but if there was some special occasion, like a party, she would often wash it, have me partly dry it in front of the lounge fire (in those days there were no domestic hair dryers for the likes of us) then wind it round and round bits of material. The next morning I would have a perfect wave but sleeping with it all trussed up was most uncomfortable.

When I was about six, I recall a lady coming to do my mother's hair. After any trimming that was needed she would put a tablet and some methylated spirits in a contraption, light it and heat some curling tongs in a frame above the flame. This was one of a few different methods to create waves, a fashion worn by many women who had their hair cut to just below their ears.

By the time I went to the Convent School the fringe, still taken over to one side, was held by a Bakelite slide instead of the bow. Apart from the slides having to be tortoiseshell, there were no rules about how hair should be worn, with some girls having natural curls which they often allowed to grow long to fall over their shoulders. Plaits were also popular.

Around that time my Mother secured a part time job in the local library. With the increased family income she was able to use a small salon some ten minutes walk from the house. Run by two exceedingly nice ladies, they had much more advanced equipment than was used by Mum's former travelling hairdresser. Being older (it was around 1943), I was growing my hair longer and taking more interest in my appearance. For some time I'd been an avid reader of 'The Picturegoer' Magazine, a weekly magazine priced at three old pence (1.25p) and was influenced by the styles of the film stars of the day.

The two ladies were up-to-date with all the cutting and setting techniques. What's more they were able to persuade my Mum to let me have the style I wanted. One craze involved sweeping up and holding the hair with a 'kirbygrip' (still sold today in more advanced form that doesn't stick to your head). This involved inserting the grip in a tube looking like a fountain pen. Roughly two inches of damp hair was wrapped round the 'pen' and rolled up as far as it would go. When reaching the top, the tube was removed to leave the grip in position. The resulting effect was called a 'bang'. With the side 'bangs' in place the rest of the hair was turned under at the back, the overall effect being titled 'pageboy'. This was made famous by June Allyson. The 'Veronica Lake' look followed – hair left long and parted to one side, gently waved and hanging over one eye.

The ladies were happy to continue giving my Mum 'perms' every six months. When we first went, she was attached to a machine by numerous wires hanging down from what looked to me like a large lamp holder. All these wires were fixed to her hair and when the machine was turned on you could literally see steam rising. Later one of them, a Miss Myers who seemed old to me but, like the girl I replaced to take my first job, was probably in her early thirties, explained that they had a new device which did away with the wires.

I was persuaded to let her have a go on me, and it was the one and only perm I had for many a year. The whole process took three hours, one of which was sitting with heavy roller-type plugs kept in position with hair clips weighing down on my head. The result was very curly and I was glad when the curls started to drop out and I returned to my metal curling pins.

In the salons during and towards the end of the War hair was still set with rollers and pin clips, but the victim's head was placed under an electric dryer. More streamlined editions are still used in establishments today but gradually, the alternative of blow drying was introduced. Not many of us teenagers braved the salons except perhaps for a hair cut. We washed it ourselves, set it with the rollers and clips then sat in front of the fire to dry it. There were hand-held dryers available but these were too expensive for most young people to buy. I eventually got one from an aunt and uncle for my twenty first birthday.

At one time, around the age of thirteen, I was tossing up whether to be a shorthand typist or a hairdresser. The firm Toni introduced a home perm kit. It comprised a box containing a bottle of a chemical solution, a small wad of tissue paper squares, a second bottle of 'neutraliser' and about 30 pink and blue plastic rollers, one colour being bigger than the other. I found it extremely useful. It was a much cheaper option than going to the salon and I developed quite a reputation, doing the hair of several of my friends and their mothers. In fact I tried it out on one of my friends before deciding to use it myself.

Although I neither wanted nor received payment, I was frequently invited to their homes for tea. Margaret, my particular friend, had two gorgeous brothers. The family traded in greengrocery at Smithfield Market in the centre of Manchester and I remember in particular enjoying the first of the season's English tomatoes. In those days you only got fruit and vegetables that were in season, sadly changed so far as I'm concerned, with the advent of supermarkets. When I first came to live in France it was a great treat to go back to that way of living with weekly street markets and nearly everyone having their own vegetable patch. We do have supermarkets but produce is ninety-nine per cent grown in France.

Digressing into history for a moment, it would seem that heat has been used for hair curling since the appearance of the first tongs in the eighteen seventies. They were tested to confirm the right temperature by holding them on a newspaper to see if they turned it brown. Charles Nessler, who died in 1952 is accredited with an invention launched in 1905 involving an electric heating device, cow urine and water. After two failed tests on his wife, burning hair off and leaving scalp wounds, an improved model appeared in London in 1909. Spanish, Swiss, Czech, German, French inventors, no doubt amongst others, all men, entered the field, many with the heated rollers hanging from a complex system of wires and all seeking to curl without burning.

Toni were first to produce the home 'permanent wave' kit. After washing the hair and partially drying it to leave it damp, strands were dipped into the chemical solution then, covered by a square of the tissue paper, wrapped over or under the pink curlers, and left for about thirty minutes. The trick was to ensure enough time for the chemical to work, and I would unwrap the first curler to see if the hair stayed in place. If and when it did, all the others were removed and the neutraliser was applied, left about ten minutes then washed off with shampoo. A sit in front of an open fire dried out the curls which stayed in 'permanently' and the house would smell of the chemical for ages.

Toni advertised the product using twins, one girl with and one without the treatment. The phrase 'I'm giving myself a Toni this weekend' entered the English language and women continued to use them for many years. Similar products appeared on the market such as Prom, Lilt, Rayve, Bobbi and Shadow Wave, often using actresses like Lucille Ball in their adverts. I believe the system is still available today, although not under the old names. I have a few of the pink curlers tucked away somewhere.

In later years I became known for trying whatever style came into fashion. One, the 'cap cut' required trimming all over to within two inches of the scalp, shaped around the face to give an 'elfin' look. When I first had it, the shock had barely worn off before I got home to be confronted by Mum. She couldn't believe her eyes. I was beginning to sink under her criticism when my elder Brother came to the rescue. The moment he entered the kitchen he said it was the best he'd ever seen me. That calmed things down until my Father arrived and asked who the 'boy' was. At work, for a time I achieved celebrity status, reactions being in the main favourable, although there were some against.

Like most women, the love hate relationship with hair continues to this day. I'm surprised more of us don't end up as bald as some of our menfolk. At the time there was little fashion related to their styles. The customary short back and sides, regulation for service personnel, was the order of the day. There was 'Brylcreem'. Dashing airmen in uniform could be seen grinning down from posters, in magazines and at the cinema with their dark hair smoothed flat with the stuff.

In the pre-electric gadget age, shaving of the masculine beard was an art. Until razor blades and 'safety razors' were introduced, most used the cut throat type instruments still operated in barbers' shops. During the war, the blades were in short supply and often came in packets of five. They would be carefully inserted in metal holders which became more sophisticated as time went by. Shaving soap was a must, generally applied by brush and here again manufacturers competed to produce the best brush. I recall one up-market present handed down by my Father to my husband. Called the Rolls razor, it was housed in an ornate metal box with base of slate used to sharpen it.

Eyes.

In 'elementary school' (what we now call junior) our eyes had to be tested every twelve to eighteen months. I'd kept quiet about having trouble doing my homework , needing to squint under electric light to see figures clearly, but at the age of eight my parents were summoned to the head teacher. It was decided that I needed glasses, or 'specs' as they are now called. Apparently I was entitled to free steel frames but Mum and Dad, no doubt noting my concern, decided to seek something nicer.

An appointment was made and I duly attended the optician at Lewis's Department Store. Following another test he produced two or three different shaped pairs. It seemed I was stuck either with the free metal rims similar to those sometimes worn by late comedian Les Dawson or 'horn rimmed' ones with tortoiseshell frames. We chose what I felt was the least damaging pair and I hated them.

Inevitably at school I had to suffer the usual ridicule with boys calling slogans such as 'speccy four eyes' after me. In those days spectacles were an affliction and only after I was married did come to terms with wearing them. By then they were beginning to be treated as universal fashion accessories.

In the nineteen sixties I was daft enough to choose what I thought was a rather striking purple pair which, combined with my then thick lenses caused my son to call me 'Biggles' – a title I've had to live with ever since. I have a Biggles teddy bear and recently became the possessor of a Biggles key ring, bought for me by my son from the War Memorial Museum.

Make up

I was too young for make up during the first three years of the War. Most girls were not allowed to use it until they were well into their teens and it was in short supply anyway. By the time I was fifteen, my friend Pam was dating a boy called John, much to the disapproval of her parents. She first met him after one of our Women's' Junior Air Corps (WJACs) meetings which ended as his Air Training Corps sessions began. He had a red-headed companion who took a shine to me.

Unbeknown to me, my friend arranged for us to meet them both outside the cinema on one of our trips. When I called for her she was wearing cream powder and lipstick. She offered me some, and I cautiously accepted. The date was a disaster. I just didn't fancy him at all and I'm ashamed to say that, at that age, it probably showed. I don't even remember the boy's name. On second thoughts I do, but I won't mention it... it wasn't his fault, well not completely.

Undeterred, Pam arranged for me to meet Roy, again as a means of her keeping an assignation with her John. Roy was slightly better than the red head (although I didn't have anything against red heads, at least I think I didn't, but who knows at that age). We went to Belle Vue motor cycle speedway circuit, a typical oval cinder track constructed in the American style. Surrounded by stands, was big enough to accommodate a football pitch in the centre and the stadium survived until its demolition after the 'last stock car race' on 14th November 1987. Well known riders were competing and I really enjoyed myself. There were several repeat visits, until Pam split up with John. That meant there was no need of the foursome, so I had to let Roy down as gently as possible, telling him that unfortunately I was very busy.

I suppose being one of four boys, my Father was old fashioned and didn't let me wear make up until I was seventeen (little did he know). Only then did he relent at the insistence of my Mother. For Christmas, she bought me some Coty vanishing cream and a box of face powder together with a small box of Bourjois Rouge. I was always very pale and used to get asked if I was ill. Mother felt I needed some colour.

The first time my Father noticed it he asked if I'd stuck my face in a flour bag. This didn't do much for my self confidence and I often considered I was plain, especially because of the glasses - my habit of picking pretty and attractive friends didn't help either. My favourite films always featured an ugly duckling character who turned out to be a swan.

I'm sure I wouldn't have won a beauty competition but looking back I suppose I couldn't have been all that bad. By the age of seventeen, a number of boy friends had bitten the dust and a fairly steady stream continued until my wedding in 1955. There were some heart breaks on the way and three failed proposals of marriage.

CHAPTER 10

MUSIC

Classic and modern

In our house, music was important. It was more than important. My mother was a soprano soloist with the 'Manchester Cathedral Craddocks' Mixed Choir'. The Principal, Mr. Craddock was a proud man. He steadfastly refused to compete in Music Festivals, declaring he had nothing to prove. He claimed that his choir was the best - each performance confirmed it. That was until, goaded by two rival conductors, he gave in.

The choir was entered in the Southport Musical Festival, one of the most prestigious of the time. I can still remember my Mother's pride when she returned home from the event to announce that they had won first prize. The victory increased their popularity and they went on to give many performances. Two were in famous Manchester Halls, the one the Houldsworth (still going) and the other the Free Trade Hall (now a Radisson luxury hotel).

Until 1943, we had one of the old HMV Cabinet 'gramophones'. My job was to turn the side mounted handle to rewind the clockwork mechanism which kept the turntable going. It was always apparent when this was needed because the records began to slow, slurring the music or voices of the singers. Then my brother appeared with an electric motor which he inserted, eliminating my handle turning duties. Being good with his hands he also attached an arm which allowed up to three records to be played, one after the other.

My parents concentrated on classical orchestral recordings or well known performers of the day such as Caruso, Peter Dawson or Heddle Nash. With money tight, new records weren't often bought and my father spent many a lunch hour searching for bargains in second hand shops. My brother, aged sixteen and a half at the start of the Second World War, was developing an interest in dance music, saving up for renditions by Tommy Dorsey, Glen Miller, and various female singers. He shared a passion for Bing Crosby with my mother, but wasn't too fond of Vera Lynne.

By the fifties Frank Sinatra stole my heart despite the family accusing me of just wanting to be different. One of my great memories was of his Manchester visit to the Palace Theatre, just after the war ended. Somehow I managed to get a ticket. 'Bobby-soxers' were all the rage – American girls who congregated to mob performers such as Sinatra, Frankie Laine and Johnny Ray. Needless to say the habit crossed the Atlantic.

The 'Bobby-soxers' were at the Palace Theatre concert, making their usual noise. After the first few minutes of his performance, with many of them in front, jumping up and down screaming their hearts out, Frank stopped the band. I don't know what he said to the girls, but they were quiet for the rest of the concert allowing us all to enjoy the music. Sinatra magnetism, as well as his superb voice, came over much better in the flesh. We weren't used to big American performers and being able to listen to my then current favourite was better than all the recordings or radio broadcasts. There was no stereo or popular television at the time to compete with live shows. It was also good to have singers capable of and determined to perform without a barrage of noise coupled with the bouncing about so often encouraged in pop concerts today.

Singing lessons

Towards the end of the war, when air raids were no longer a threat, directors and producers were starting to put on musicals, concentrating upon the old established favourites. Mother took me to see a matinee performance of 'The Maid of the Mountains' also at the Palace Theatre. Aged sixteen it started me off on a lifelong love of musical shows. Manchester was fortunate in that it gained the reputation of providing discerning audiences. When producers became more courageous after the end of the war, we were privileged with one or two month runs of South Pacific, Carousel, Annie Get Your Gun and others prior to their making the London stages.

The partners in the firm where I worked at the time, as the Christmas treat for the staff, provided a meal then took us to one of the musicals. For me, this was a much better celebration than some of the office parties I suffered later. To popular acclaim the event was moved to the end of January after a year or two and helped liven up what was often a dreary month.

It was accepted that I should follow in my mother's vocal footsteps after my school discovered I had a 'pleasant' voice. Introduced to my first singing teacher at the age of fifteen, whilst the war was still raging, I stayed with her until her retirement two years later. Lessons were once a week and started with the laborious practice of scales in various octaves, both during the initial lessons and at home. My teacher also tried to expand my piano playing beyond the Grade 1 exam I'd passed at the age of ten, but singing was my passion.

I never attained my brother Norman's standard. He was fast becoming an accomplished pianist. Whilst he could play without, he would still frequent City centre music stores such as Hime & Addison or Forsythes when he could afford to buy from the hundreds of printed sheets of music on display. If a piece was not available, they would always order it. In importance I suspect this part of their businesses rivalled the sales of the musical instruments they marketed at the time. The range could be compared to the rows of DVDs and CDs available today, only then, the piece had to be taken home and learnt – a much greater task than just sliding it into a machine and letting the electronics do the work. Some would say a far more rewarding achievement as well. 'Records' were also on sale of course and were growing in popularity. High Street stores like Lewis's had booths in their music departments equipped with headphones where buyers could listen before choosing their purchase, but the dedicated sheet music shops could still hold their own, most larger British towns boasting at least one that sold nothing else.

I dropped piano lessons after one term to concentrate on singing. My first music teacher away from school, Miss Taylor, worked from home and lived only a five minute walk from our house. Most lessons were in the early evening after work and like so many of her counterparts throughout the country, she taught in her front sitting room, which housed the upright piano. She kept hard backed song books featuring many of the classical composers and we would practice a chosen piece during the lesson. She would let me take a book home to continue practising in our lounge.

My Mother seemed to like change and would frequently surprise us by having the cleaning lady help her swap the dining room with the lounge whilst we were out, but the piano always stayed in the alcove by the fireplace. It was an important, if not the most important item of furniture.

I really enjoyed my singing and always looked forward to the lessons. It was quite hard work and I learned many of the techniques from Miss Taylor that allowed me to develop in later years. Amongst these was timing. Often she would set the 'metronome' above the piano. To me, it was a strange clockwork object with the mechanism encased in wood and shaped a bit like a small pyramid. One side could be unhooked and removed to reveal a slim metal rod which, when in motion ticked loudly from side to side. That set the time for the music and the speed of those rhythmic ticks could be changed by sliding a piece of lead up and down on the rod. Being clockwork, it always amused me when in the middle of a song the spring would run out of strength and the beat slow down. We would have to stop whilst my teacher restored normal service by giving the brass key at the back enough turns to wind it up again. It was sad when, one day, Miss Taylor broke the news to me that age was getting the better of her and she'd decided to give up.

Learning of my Teacher's impending retirement, my mother discovered that Tom Case, well known for his performances throughout Lancashire, had taken rooms in Manchester City Centre, not far from where I worked. Age was catching up with him and he was thinking of giving lessons to supplement income whilst he scaled down his concert work. She made an appointment for us to see him.

Arriving at his new address, we were shown into his rehearsal room to be greeted by a man of medium height, with white hair and a kindly disposition. He immediately made me feel at ease, asked me to sing a few scales and agreed to accept me as a pupil. Mr. Case was a good tutor and I progressed well, enjoying the lunch hour lessons. However, unable to overcome extreme shyness, I always held back, never able to achieve the expression and freedom that came naturally when practising at home. This must have been of concern to my parents. Father received a meagre pay packet and only later did I learn the lessons cost my parents three shillings each. This ate into the extra two or three pounds a week my Mother earned working in the local lending library.

One day I arrived early, whilst the pupil before me, a contralto, was still singing. Mr. Case called me into the practice room, inviting me to join Bernice in a duet. For some reason, whilst we were singing together, I forgot my reserve and found myself equalling my achievements at home. It was wonderful, especially when I noticed the expression of surprise on Tom Case's face.

"Where did that come from?" he demanded. "Don't ever let me hear again that sweet little voice you've been using. I knew you had more to give but I couldn't find a way to it. Now we have."

Within months he was talking of a concert at Houldsworth Hall. Two or three guest performers were to be invited, to be joined by four of his pupils. He chose me to be one of the pupils. The thrill of selection slowly turned into abject fear as the date of the performance approached. My stomach began to churn every time I thought of what I would have to do, and in the end nerves won. I was unable to take part.

Performances

Cyril Shaw, the cashier in the firm of solicitors where I worked knew of my interest in singing. He was a brilliant pianist and invited me to one of the musical evenings he and his wife held at their home. I became a regular visitor and was almost always invited to sing to his accompaniment.

Ely Topham, a professional pianist also worked in our office. His 'Topham Quintet' played each weekend at the Buxton Hydro and both men did everything they could to encourage me into a singing career. Cyril arranged an audition for me with the Carl Rosa Opera Company. The troupe were on a four week visit to Manchester Opera House shortly after the war had ended. Despite the support of both men and of my family, nerves again took over, and I chickened out.

Looking back I realise it wasn't just the fear of performing that stopped me. Like so many other teenagers, living through the constant threat of a bomb, waking up from a deep sleep to scramble into the ever ready trousers and jumper and then to rush into the shelter every time the air raid siren sounded, took its toll. Whilst that period in my life remains precious to me and I made many friends, I often wonder how different it may have been if I'd grown up in a calmer peaceful time. Surely it's not only war and conflict that brings families together. The wounds left are so difficult to heal.

Towards the end of the war years, operatic and dramatic societies were beginning to re-form. In a braver moment, my friend Margaret and I responded to a Didsbury Operatic Society advertisement. They were looking for members of the chorus for a production of 'The New Moon'. The Secretary interviewed us and announced that as we were both under the age of eighteen, we were ineligible for the chorus. However, if we had experience, we could join the dancing troupe. Naturally we confirmed we had, not mentioning that it was for a year or two, maybe three, when we were very young. It was hard going - very hard going.

Virtually at the point of collapse after six weeks, I began to understand the meaning of the phrase 'It's not what you know but who you know'. My mother knew Rhona, the dancing instructor, having worked with her on a concert. Rhona had handled the dancers and my Mum the singers. Nothing specific was said, but the Secretary called us to one side to explain that two vacancies had cropped up in the choir. If we agreed, they would bend the rules and admit us.

The Producer was very experienced; the Music Director wonderful. The Society earned a reputation for picking up new musicals as soon as they were released from the professional theatres. One of our greatest successes was 'Castles in Spain'. For the first time I began to experience the organisation and preparation for a full length show. A Manchester firm devoted to the supply of wigs and dresses for the theatrical world not only furnished the costumes, but also the make up artists. For the first couple of shows I had to work hard to overcome both nerves and embarrassment when I sat in the make up chair, for all the artists were men. David, one of the seniors took me on and I drove him mad when it came to the eyes. Whatever he did, he couldn't stop me blinking when he tried to apply mascara. He must have been a sadist, for he made a point of selecting me out of the queue every night when his chair became vacant. He learnt where I worked, and took to accompanying me to the post office with the mail in the evenings. Even when I declined his invitation for a date I still got preferential treatment.

When I first joined the Society, we had a chorus of one hundred. The majority were women, and those men who weren't fighting on the front line, mostly in their late forties or more, made up the number. Gradually as soldiers returned to 'civvy street', the balance changed more or less to equality. We also had a full orchestra, and during breaks we all used to chat. The cello player in particular took my fancy and eventually we went out together. Regrettably, for him at least, the romance was short lived. He had a very small car and it was difficult to be amorous with the thin end of a cello sticking in my back.

We performed 'Castles in Spain' at the Capital Theatre – later to become Granada TV Studios – and Eric Box, the composer, sent us a good luck telegram on the opening night. Critics from the Manchester Evening News (allied to the then Manchester Guardian), the Manchester Evening Chronicle, the Express and several local papers did us proud. The reviews were incredible, leading to a further week's booking at the Rex Theatre, Wilmslow, playing to full houses. In turn this led to the Theatre Royal, Bolton, an established venue where some of the resident staff took us for fellow professionals.

I spent nine happy years with the Company and only gave up when I got married. I also managed to overcome my nerves sufficiently to perform solo to guests at many musical evenings in friends' houses. This led to invites to sing at weddings, often in front of seventy or eighty people. Only later did I discover that my brother, in anticipation of such requests, would surreptitiously bring my music along. When invited to sing he'd always accompany me on the piano, which I suspect was the main reason I was able to do it.

It was a time when entertainment wasn't dished out on a conveyer belt as a twenty four hour commodity. Most families had their own musical evenings with pianos, accordions, and string instruments often playing their part. Community activity was greater, whether it was the church choir, the local dramatic, music or any similar group, always with the emphasis on do-it-yourself activity.

We were lucky to live through the era of the big bands. They played all the popular tunes of the day, and when new pieces achieved fame, shops were likely to have waiting lists for the printed sheets of the music the bands recorded. To many, a household was incomplete unless it had a piano, accompanied by the traditional stool. Under the hinged seat cushion of the stool would be printed music, including those popular sheets. In this, the twenty first century, larger bands and orchestras seem to be making a come-back, but they're still a long way from Carroll Gibbons, Geraldo, Harry Roy, Oscar Rabin, Edmundo Ross, Henry Hall, Billy Cotton and others of those pre-and post-war years. Then people sought out and bought sheet music and records as enthusiastically as we purchase DVDs or CDs or download today. The big difference is that then people, not machines, made music.

Song can cause or be the means of expression of great emotion. For me the most stirring event of all was VE Day (standing for Victory in Europe). In May 1945, (I think it was the 8th, although commemorating documentation was signed between the seventh and the ninth, with newspapers as usual claiming to be the first with the announcement), town and city centres throughout the land were packed with people. They cheered and laughed and broke into song. First it was the National Anthem – God Save the King, and then Land of Hope and Glory. This was followed by 'We'll Meet Again' and many other war time favourites made popular by singers such as Vera Lynn and Anne Shelton, some from the First World War.

Music has lost none of its power. The medical profession acknowledges it can treat stress and stimulate relaxation. I only wish the tradition, alive in the football grounds and on other national or international occasions, would creep back into homes. I feel that if we were more active in the making of music, family unity and cohesion would stand a better chance of survival. Listening to an outsider serving up non-stop entertainment through ear phones, the radio, TV or computer is no substitute.

INDIGO DREAMS PUBLISHING
132 HINCKLEY ROAD
STONEY STANTON
LEICS
LE9 4LN
WWW.INDIGODREAMS.CO.UK